GLEANINGS FROM THE GLORIOUS QURAN

AZIZ AHMED

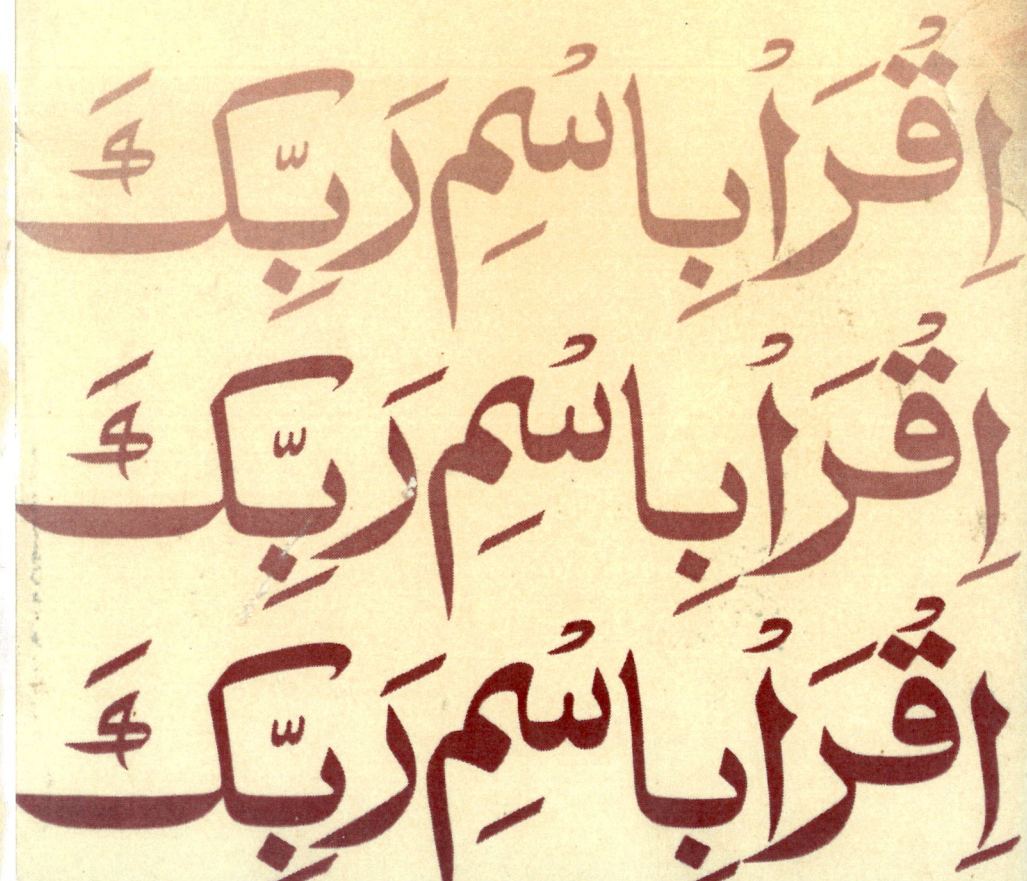

For Maureen and
Tommy
May God bless you

Aba

April 1981

GLEANINGS
FROM THE
GLORIOUS QURAN

GLEANINGS
FROM THE
GLORIOUS QURAN

AZIZ AHMED

KARACHI
OXFORD UNIVERSITY PRESS
OXFORD   NEW YORK   DELHI
1980

Oxford University Press

OXFORD LONDON GLASGOW
NEW YORK TORONTO MELBOURNE WELLINGTON
CAPE TOWN NAIROBI DAR ES SALAAM
KUALA LUMPUR SINGAPORE HONG KONG TOKYO
DELHI BOMBAY CALCUTTA MADRAS KARACHI

ISBN 0 19 577280 6

Typeset by
Saad Publications, Karachi,
Printed by
Civil & Military Press, Ltd., Karachi
Published by
Oxford University Press,
Haroon House, Dr. Ziauddin Ahmad Road,
G.P.O. Box 442, Karachi-1

PUBLISHER'S NOTE

For the convenience of the general reader, diacriticals have been omitted; they are normally inserted as follows in the names which appear in the text as listed below:

A'âd	Abî Tâlib	Abû Bakr	Abû Tâlib
Al-Amîn	Al-'Aqabah	Al-Islâm	Al-Ḥudeybiah
Al-Madînah	'Arafât	Ḥânif	Ḥirâ
Ḥunafa	Iblîs	Ibn Khaldûn	Ka'bah
Khadîjah	Muttalib	Qur'ân	Ramadân
Sûrah	Ta'if	Thamûd	

PREFACE

This is a selection of verses culled from *The Meaning of the Glorious Koran* by Mohammad Marmaduke Pickthall.[1] The Introduction that follows and the few comments that have been included are also taken from Pickthall's translation, except for one or two instances where I have quoted from *The Koran Interpreted* by Arthur J. Arberry.[2]

Both authors agree, as do many others who have attempted it, that the Quran cannot be translated. Pickthall says that he has rendered the Quran 'almost literally and every effort has been made to choose befitting language. But the result is not the Glorious Quran, that inimitable symphony, the very sounds of which move men to tears and ecstasy. It is only an attempt to present the meaning of the Quran— and peradventure something of the charm—in English. It can never take the place of the Quran in Arabic, nor is it meant to do so.'

This applies with far greater force to this brief compilation, the purpose of which is to attempt to convey to the English reader, who may not have the opportunity to read the full text of the Glorious Quran, something of its Divine Message.

To assist the lay reader to appreciate the many-faceted splendour of the Quran, I have placed the verses selected[3] under certain heads. It should be noted that the verses included here are merely illustrative, and not by any means exhaustive, of the few subjects chosen from 'the Ocean of prophetic eloquence', as Arberry describes the Holy Quran.

[1] M.M. Pickthall, *The Meaning of the Glorious Koran*, George Allen & Unwin, London, 1976. I am indebted to the publishers for permission to use Pickthall's translation.

[2] A.J. Arberry, *The Koran Interpreted*, Oxford University Press, London, 1964.

[3] The Surahs (chapters) and the verses of the Quran are numbered in this book as in Pickthall's translation; in this collection S stands for the Surah and v for the Verse.

In a thoughtful address[1] at Harvard on the conflict between the West and the East, Aleksandr Solzhenitsyn said:

> On the way from the Renaissance to our day, we have enriched our experience, but we have lost the concept of a Supreme Complete Entity which used to restrain our passions. We have placed too much hope in political and social reforms, only to find that we were being deprived of our most precious possession: our spiritual life. In the East it is destroyed by the dealings and machinations of the ruling party. In the West commercial interests tend to suffocate it. This is the real crisis. The split in the world is less terrible than the similarity of the disease plaguing its main areas.

It is the writer's hope and prayer that this collection of verses from the Glorious Quran may serve as a reminder to those who can find time for reflection, despite the pressures of modern life, to seek also to serve their Creator in their daily lives and to endeavour to help preserve spiritual values in the face of the onslaught of materialism sweeping the world.

January 1980   AZIZ AHMED

---

[1] *Harvard Commencement,* June 1978.

CONTENTS

INTRODUCTION[1]

MUHAMMAD, son of Abdullah, son of Abdul Muttalib, of the tribe of Qureysh, was born at Mecca fifty-three years before the Hijrah. His father died before he was born, and he was protected first by his grandfather, Abdul Muttalib, and, after his grandfather's death, by his uncle, Abu Talib. As a young boy he travelled with his uncle in the merchants' caravan to Syria, and some years afterwards made the same journey in the service of a wealthy widow named Khadijah. So faithfully did he transact the widow's business, and so excellent was the report of his behaviour which she received from her old servant who had accompanied him, that she soon afterwards married her young agent; and the marriage proved a very happy one, though she was fifteen years older than he was. Throughout the twenty-six years of their life together he remained devoted to her; and after her death, when he took other wives he always mentioned her with the greatest love and reverence. This marriage gave him rank among the notables of Mecca, while his conduct earned for him the surname *Al-Amin*, the 'trustworthy'.

The Meccans claimed descent from Abraham through Ishmael, and tradition stated that their temple, the Kabah, had been built by Abraham for the worship of the One God. It was still called the House of Allah, but the chief objects of worship there were a number of idols which were called daughters of Allah and intercessors. The few who felt disgust at this idolatry, which had prevailed for centuries, longed for the religion of Abraham and tried to find out what had been its teaching. Such seekers of the truth were known as Hunafa (sing: Hanif), a word originally meaning 'those who turn away' (from the existing idol-worship), but coming in the end to have the sense of 'upright' or 'by nature upright', because such persons held the way of truth to be right

---

[1] Extracted from Pickthall's Introduction to *The Meaning of the Glorious Koran*.

conduct. These Hunafa did not form a community. They were the agnostics of their day, each seeking truth by the light of his own inner consciousness. Muhammad son of Abdullah became one of these. It was his practice to retire for a month of every year to a cave in the desert for medita-

The First revelation (A.D. 610) tion. His place of retreat was Hira,[1] a desert hill not far from Mecca, and his chosen month was Ramadan, the month of heat. It was there one night toward the end of his quiet month that the first revelation came to him when he was forty years old. He was asleep or in a trance[2] when he heard a voice say: 'Read!' He said: 'I cannot read.' The voice again said: 'Read!' He said: 'I cannot read.' A third time the voice, more terrible, commanded: 'Read!' He said: 'What can I read?' The voice said:

> Read: In the name of the Lord who createth,
> Createth man from a clot.
> Read: And thy Lord is the Most Bounteous,
> Who teacheth by the pen,
> Teacheth man that which he knew not.[3]

When he awoke the words remained 'as if inscribed upon his heart'. He went out of the cave on to the hillside and heard the same awe-inspiring voice say: 'O Muhammad! Thou art Allah's messenger, and I am Gabriel.' Then he

The Vision of Mt. Hira raised his eyes and saw the angel, in the likeness of a man, standing in the sky above the horizon. And again the dreadful voice said: 'O Muhammad! Thou art Allah's messenger, and I am Gabriel.' Muhammad (God bless and keep him!) stood quite still, turning away his face from the brightness of the vision, but whithersoever he might turn his face, there always stood the angel confronting him. He remained thus a long while till at length the angel vanished, when he returned in great distress of mind to his wife Khadijah. She did her best to reassure him, saying that his conduct had been such that Allah would not let a harmful spirit come to him and that it was her hope that he was to become the Prophet of his people. On their return to Mecca she took him

---

1 Strictly speaking, Hira is the name of the cave and the hill is called *Jabel-el-Noor*, the Mountain of Light.

2 According to some authorities he was in meditation.

3 S. XCVI, vv. 1-5.

to her cousin Waraqa ibn Naufal, a very old man, who knew the Scriptures of the Jews and Christians, who declared his belief that the heavenly messenger who came to Moses of old had come to Muhammad, and that he was chosen as the Prophet of his people.

To understand the reason of the Prophet's diffidence and his extreme distress of mind after the vision of Mt. Hira, His distress of mind it must be remembered that the Hunafa, of whom he had been one, sought true religion in the natural and regarded with distrust the intercourse with spirits of which men 'avid of the Unseen',[1] sorcerers and soothsayers and even poets, boasted in those days. Moreover, he was a man of humble disposition and devout intelligence, a lover of quiet and solitude, and the very thought of being chosen out of all mankind to face mankind, alone, with such a Message, appalled him at the first. Recognition of the Divine nature of the call he had received involved a change in his whole mental outlook sufficiently disturbing to a sensitive and honest mind, and also the forsaking of his quiet, honoured way of life. The early biographers tell how his wife Khadijah 'tried the spirit' which came to him and proved it to be good, and how, with the continuance of the revelations and the conviction that they brought, he at length accepted the tremendous task imposed on him, becoming filled with an enthusiasm of obedience which justifies his proudest title of 'The Slave of Allah'.

For the first three years or rather less, of his Mission, the Prophet preached only to his family and his intimate friends, while the people of Mecca as a whole regarded him as one who had become a little mad. The first of all his converts First converts was his wife Khadijah, the second his first cousin Ali, whom he had adopted, the third his servant Zeyd, a former slave. His old friend Abu Bakr also was among those early converts with some of his slaves and dependents.

At the end of the third year the Prophet received the

---

[1] S. LXXXI, vv. 22-24 refer to the Prophet's vision at Mount Hira thus:
And your comrade is not mad,
Surely he beheld him on the clear horizon.
And he is not avid of the Unseen.

command to 'arise and warn',[1] whereupon he began to
Beginning of persecution preach in public, pointing out the wretched folly of idolatry
in face of the tremendous laws of day and night, of life and
death, of growth and decay, which manifest the power of
Allah and attest His sovereignty. It was then, when he began
to speak against their gods, that Qureysh became actively
hostile, persecuting his poorer disciples, mocking and insul-
ting him.

The converts of the first four years were mostly humble
folk unable to defend themselves against oppression. So
cruel was the persecution they endured that the Prophet
The flight to Abyssinia advised all who could possibly contrive to do so to emigrate
to a Christian country, Abyssinia. And still in spite of persecution and emigration the little company of Muslims grew
in number. Qureysh were seriously alarmed. The idol worship
at the Kabah, the holy place to wnich all Arabia made
pilgrimage, ranked for them, as guardians of the Kabah, as
first among their vested interests. At the season of the
pilgrimage they posted men on all the roads to warn the
tribes against the madman who was preaching in their midst.
They tried to bring the Prophet to a compromise, offering to
accept his religion if he would so modify it as to make room
for their gods as intercessors with Allah, offering to make
him their king if he would give up attacking idolatry; but
their efforts at negotiation failed.

Conversion of Omar The exasperation of the idolaters was increased by the
conversion of Omar, one of their stalwarts. They grew
The Prophet and his clan ostracised more and more embittered, till things came to such a pass
that they decided to ostracise the Prophet's whole clan,
idolaters who protected him as well as Muslims who believed
in him.

Then, for three years, the Prophet was shut up with all his
kinsfolk in their stronghold which situated in one of
the gorges which run down to Mecca. Only at the time of

---

[1] S. LXXIV, vv. 1-5 contain this command:
O thou enveloped in thy cloak,
Arise and warn!
Thy Lord magnify,
Thy raiment purify,
Pollution shun!

pilgrimage could he go out and preach, or did any of his kinsfolk dare to go into the city.

At the season of the yearly pilgrimage, the prophet came upon a little group of men who heard him gladly. They came from Yathrib, a city more than two hundred miles away, which has since become world-famous as Al-Madinah, 'the city' *par excellence.* The men from Yathrib

At Yathrib there were Jewish tribes with learned rabbis, who had often spoken to the pagans of a Prophet soon to come among the Arabs, with whom, when he came, the Jews would destroy the pagans as the tribes of Aad and Thamud had been destroyed of old for their idolatry. When the men from Yathrib saw Muhammad they recognised him as the Prophet whom the Jewish rabbis had described to them.

In the following year, at the time of pilgrimage seventy-three Muslims from Yathrib came to Mecca to vow allegiance to the Prophet and invite him to their city. At Al-Aqabah by night they swore to defend him as they would defend their own wives and children. It was then that the Hijrah, the Flight to Yathrib, was decided. Second pact of Al-Aqabah

Soon the Muslims who were in a position to do so began to sell their property and to leave Mecca unobtrusively. Qureysh had wind of what was going on. They hated Muhammad in their midst, but dreaded what he might become if he escaped from them. It would be better, they considered, to destroy him now. The death of Abu Talib had removed his chief protector; but still they had to reckon with the vengeance of his clan upon the clan of the murderer. They cast lots and chose a slayer out of every clan. All these were to attack the Prophet simultaneously and strike together as one man. Thus his blood would be on all Qureysh. It was at this time (Ibn Khaldun asserts, and it is the only explanation of what happened afterwards) that the Prophet received the first revelation ordering him to make war upon his persecutors 'until persecution is no more and religion is for Allah only'.[1] Plot to murder the Prophet

[1] S. VIII, v. 39 which reads:
 And fight them until persecution is no more, and religion is all for Allah. But if they cease, then lo! Allah is Seer of what they do.

The last of the able Muslims to remain in Mecca were
Abu Bakr, Ali and the Prophet himself. Abu Bakr, a man
of wealth, had bought two riding-camels and retained a
guide in readiness for the Flight. The Prophet only waited
God's command. It came at length. It was the night appointed for his murder. The slayers were before his house. He
gave his cloak to Ali, bidding him lie down on the bed so
that anyone looking in might think Muhammad lay there.
The slayers were to strike him as he came out of the house,
whether in the night or early morning. He knew they would
not injure Ali. Then he left the house and, it is said, a blindness fell upon the would-be murderers so that he put dust on
their heads as he passed by—without their knowing it. He
went to Abu Bakr's house and called to him, and the two
went together to a cavern[1] in the desert hills and hid there
till the hue and cry was past, Abu Bakr's son and daughter
and his herdsman bringing them food and tidings after
nightfall. Once a search-party came quite near them in their
The HIJRAH hiding-place, and Abu Bakr was afraid; but the Prophet
(June 20, said: 'Fear not! Allah is with us'.[2] Then, when the coast was
A.D. 622) clear, Abu Bakr had the riding-camels and the guide brought
to the cave one night, and they set out on the long ride to
Yathrib.

Such was the Hijrah, the Flight from Mecca to Yathrib,
which counts as the beginning of the Muslim era. The thir-
teen years of humiliation, of persecution, of seeming failure,
of prophecy still unfulfilled, were over. The ten years of
success, the fullest that has ever crowned one man's endeavour, had begun.

Unparalleled In those ten years the Prophet destroyed idolatry in
success Arabia; raised woman from the status of a chattel to complete legal equality with man; effectually stopped the
drunkenness and immorality which had till then disgraced
the Arabs; made men in love with faith, sincerity and honest
dealing; transformed tribes who had been for centuries
content with ignorance into a people with the greatest thirst

1 Called THAWR.
2 S. IX, v. 40 which reads:
...He said unto his comrade: Grieve not. Lo! Allah is with us. Then Allah
caused His peace of reassurance to descend upon him...

for knowledge; and for the first time in history made universal human brotherhood a fact and principle of common law. And his support and guide in all that work was the Koran.

The Hijrah makes a clear division in the story of the Prophet's Mission, which is evident in the Koran. Till then he had been a preacher only. Thenceforth he was the ruler of a state, at first a very small one, which grew in ten years to the empire of Arabia. The kind of guidance which he and his people needed after the Hijrah was not the same as that which they had before needed. The latter gave guidance to the individual soul and to the Prophet as warner; the former gave guidance to a growing social and political community and to the Prophet as example, lawgiver and reformer.

In the seventh year of the Hijrah, the Prophet led a campaign against Kheybar, the stronghold of the Jewish tribes in North Arabia, which had become a hornets' nest of his enemies.

It was at Kheybar that a Jewess prepared for the Prophet *Attempt to* poisoned meat, of which he only tasted a morsel without *Poison the* swallowing it, then warned his comrades that it was poisoned. *Prophet* One Muslim, who had already swallowed a mouthful, died immediately, and the Prophet himself, from the mere taste of it, derived the illness which eventually caused his death. The woman who had cooked the meat was brought before him. When she said that she had done it on account of the humiliation of her people, he forgave her.

In the same year the Prophet's vision[1] was fulfilled: he visited the holy place at Mecca unopposed. In accordance *Pilgrimage* with the terms of the truce (of Al-Hudeybiah) the idolaters *to Mecca* evacuated the city, and from the surrounding heights watched the procedure of the Muslims. At the end of the stipulated three days the chiefs of Qureysh sent word to remind the

[1] The Prophet saw the vision a year earlier in which he found himself entering the holy place at Mecca unopposed for Pilgrimage. A reference to this vision occurs in S. XLVIII, v. 27 which reads:

Allah has fulfilled the vision for His messenger in very truth. Ye shall indeed enter the Inviolable Place of Worship, if Allah will, secure, (having your hair) shaven and cut, not fearing. But He knoweth that which ye know not, and hath given you a near victory beforehand.

Prophet that the time was up. He then withdrew, and the idolaters reoccupied the city.

Truce broken by Qureysh In the eighth year of the Hijrah, Qureysh broke the truce by attacking a tribe that was in alliance with the Prophet and massacred them even in the sanctuary at Mecca.

Conquest of Mecca Then the Prophet summoned all the Muslims capable of bearing arms and marched to Mecca. Qureysh were over-awed. Their cavalry put up a show of defence before the town, but were routed without bloodshed; and the Prophet entered his native city as conqueror. The inhabitants expected vengeance for their past misdeeds. The Prophet proclaimed a general amnesty. Only a few known criminals were proscribed, and most of those were in the end forgiven. In their relief and surprise, the whole population of Mecca hastened to swear allegiance. The Prophet caused all the idols which were in the sanctuary to be destroyed, saying: 'Truth hath come; darkness hath vanished away', and the Muslim call to prayer was heard in Mecca.

The farewell pilgrimage In the tenth year of the Hijrah the Prophet went to Mecca as a pilgrim for the last time—his 'pilgrimage of farewell', it is called—when from Mt. Arafat he preached to an enormous throng of pilgrims. He reminded them of all the duties Al-Islam enjoined upon them, and that they would one day have to meet their Lord, who would judge each one of them according to his work. At the end of the discourse, he asked: 'Have I not conveyed the Message?' And from that great multitude of men who a few months or years before had all been conscienceless idolaters the shout went up: 'O Allah! Yes!' The Prophet said: 'O Allah! Be Thou witness!'

Illness and death of the Prophet (A.D. 632) It was during that last pilgrimage that the surah entitled *Succour*[1] was revealed, which he received as an announcement of approaching death. Soon after his return to Al-Madinah he fell ill. The tidings of his illness caused dismay throughout Arabia and anguish to the folk of Al-Madinah, Mecca and Taif, the hometowns. At early dawn on the last day of his earthly life he came out from his room beside the mosque at Al-Madinah and joined the public prayer, which Abu Bakr had been leading since his illness. And there

1 See p. 14, S. CX.

was great relief among the people, who supposed him well again. When, later in the day, the rumour grew that he was dead, Omar threatened those who spread the rumour with dire punishment, declaring it a crime to think that the Messenger of God could die. He was storming at the people in that strain when Abu Bakr came into the mosque and overheard him. Abu Bakr went to the chamber of his daughter Ayeshah, where the Prophet lay. Having ascertained the fact, and kissed the dead man's forehead, he went back into the mosque. The people were still listening to Omar, who was saying that the rumour was a wicked lie, that the Prophet who was all in all to them could not be dead. Abu Bakr went up to Omar and tried to stop him by a whispered word. Then, finding he would pay no heed, Abu Bakr called to the people, who, recognising his voice, left Omar and came crowding round him. He first gave praise to Allah, and then said: 'O people! Lo! as for him who used to worship Muhammad, Muhammad is dead. But as for him who used to worship Allah, Allah is Alive and dieth not.' He then recited the verse of the Koran:

Muhammad is but a messenger, messengers (the like of whom) have passed away before him. Will it be that, when he dieth or is slain, ye will turn back on your heels? He who turneth back on his heels doth no hurt to Allah, and Allah will reward the thankful.[1]

'And,' says the narrator, an eye-witness, 'it was as if the people had not known that such a verse had been revealed till Abu Bakr recited it.' And another witness tells how Omar used to say: 'Directly I heard Abu Bakr recite that verse my feet were cut from beneath me and I fell to the ground, for I knew that Allah's messenger was dead. May Allah bless and keep him!'

[1] S. III, v. 144.

1

THE QURAN

In the name of Allah, The Merciful, The Compassionate

Pickthall notes that the first revelation was received by the Prophet
on Mt. Hira. And because the angel bade him 'Read!'—insisted on
his 'Reading' though he was illiterate—the Sacred Book is known as
Al-Quran, 'the Reading', the Reading of the man who knew not how
to read. The arrangement of the Surahs in the Quran does not follow
the order in which they were revealed. Regarding the compilation of
the Quran, Pickthall continues:

All the Surahs of the Quran had been recorded in writing
before the Prophet's death, and many Muslims had com-
mitted the whole Quran to memory. But the written
Surahs were dispersed among the people; and...during
the Caliphate of Abu Bakr—that is to say, within two years
of the Prophet's death...a collection of the whole Quran
was made and put in writing. In the Caliphate of Othman,
A.D. 644-56, all existing copies of Surahs were called in,
and an authoritative version, based on Abu Bakr's collection and the testimony of those who had the whole Quran
by heart, was compiled exactly in the present form and
order, which is regarded as traditional and as the arrangement of the Prophet himself, the Caliph Othman and his
helpers being Comrades of the Prophet and the most
devout students of the revelation. The Quran has thus been
very carefully preserved.[1]

On the subject of this arrangement, Arberry has this to say:[2]

The reader of the Koran, particularly if he has to depend
upon a version, however accurate linguistically, is certain
to be puzzled and dismayed by the apparently random
nature of many of the Suras. This famous inconsequence
has often been attributed to clumsy patchwork on the part

[1] See Introduction to Pickthall, *The Meaning of the Glorious Koan,* p. xxviii.
[2] See Arberry, *The Koran Interpreted,* p. xi.

of the first editors. I believe it to be rather of the very
nature of the Book itself. In many passages it is stated that
the Koran had been sent down 'confirming what was
before it', by which was meant the Torah and the Gospel;
the contents of the Jewish and Christian scriptures, excep-
ting such falsifications as had been introduced into them,
were therefore taken as true and known. All truth was thus
present simultaneously within the Prophet's enraptured
soul; all truth, however fragmented, revealed itself in his
inspired utterance. The reader of the Muslim scriptures
must strive to attain the same all-embracing apprehension.
The sudden fluctuations of theme and mood will then no
longer present such difficulties as have bewildered critics
ambitious to measure the ocean of prophetic eloquence
with the thimble of pedestrian analysis. Each Sura will
now be seen to be a unity within itself, and the whole
Koran will be recognized as a single revelation, self consis-
tent to the highest degree. Though half a mortal life-time
was needed for the message to be received and communi-
cated, the message itself, being of the eternal, is one
message in eternity, however heterogeneous its temporal
expression may appear to be.

In the same context, Arberry writes of 'the astonishing wealth
and variety of rhetoric and rhythm' in the Quran, which, unlike pre-
vious translations, he has tried to capture in his rendering of it, so
that 'some faint impression may be given of its dramatic impact and
most moving beauty'. He has tried to produce, he says, something
'echoing the sublime rhetoric of the Arabic Koran', and adds: 'I have
been at pains to study its intricate and richly varied rhythms which—
apart from the message—constitute the Koran's undeniable claim to
rank among the greatest literary masterpieces of mankind.' He con-
cludes on a movingly personal note:

This task (of interpretation) was undertaken, not lightly,
and carried through to its conclusion at a time of great
personal distress, through which it comforted and sustain-
ed the writer in a manner for which he will always be
grateful. He therefore acknowledges his gratitude to
whatever power or Power inspired the man and the Prophet who first recited these scriptures.[1]

1 See Arberry, *The Koran Interpreted*, p. xii.

The Opening

In the name of Allah, the Beneficent, the Merciful.

Praise be to Allah, Lord of the Worlds,
The Beneficent, the Merciful.
Owner of the Day of Judgment,
Thee (alone) we worship; Thee (alone) we ask for help.
Show us the straight path,
The path of those whom Thou hast favoured; Not (the path) of those who earn Thine anger nor of those who go astray.

S. I, vv. 1-7

Arberry renders this magnificent Surah more exquisitely thus:

In the Name of God, the merciful, the compassionate

Praise belongs to God, the Lord of all Being,
the All-merciful, the All-compassionate,
the Master of the Day of Doom.
Thee only we serve; to Thee alone we pray for succour.
Guide us in the straight path,
the path of those whom Thou hast blessed,
not of those against whom Thou art wrathful,
nor of those who are astray.[1]

S. I, vv. 1-9

According to Pickthall, this Surah has been named by some 'The Essence of the Koran'; it has been called the Lord's Prayer of the Muslims and is an essential part of all Muslim worship, public or private.

A Divine Revelation

This is the Scripture whereof there is no doubt, a guidance unto those who ward off (evil).

Who believe in the Unseen, and establish worship, and spend of that We have bestowed upon them;

And who believe in that which is revealed unto thee (Muhammad) and that which was revealed before thee, and are certain of the Hereafter.

These depend on guidance from their Lord. These are the successful.

---

[1] See Arberry, *The Koran Interpreted*, p. 1.

As for the disbelievers, whether thou warn them or thou warn them not it is all one for them; they believe not.

Allah hath sealed their hearing and their hearts, and on their eyes there is a covering. Theirs will be an awful doom.

S. II, vv. 2-7

And if ye are in doubt concerning that which We reveal unto Our slave (Muhammad), then produce a Surah of the like thereof, and call your witnesses beside Allah if ye are truthful.

And if ye do it not—and ye can never do it—then guard yourselves against the Fire prepared for disbelievers, whose fuel is of men and stones.

S. II, vv. 23, 24

And this Quran is not such as could ever be invented in despite of Allah; but it is a confirmation of that which was before it and an exposition of that which is decreed for mankind—Therein is no doubt—from the Lord of the Worlds.

Or say they: He hath invented it? Say: Then bring a Surah like unto it, and call (for help) on all ye can besides Allah, if ye are truthful.

Nay, but they denied that, the knowledge whereof they could not compass, and whereof the interpretation (in events) hath not yet come unto them. Even so did those before them deny. Then see what was the consequence for the wrong-doers!

S. X, vv. 37-39

We have not revealed unto thee (Muhammad) this Quran that thou shouldst be distressed,

But as a reminder unto him who feareth,

A revelation from Him Who created the earth and the high heavens,

The Beneficent One, Who is established on the Throne.

S. XX, vv. 2-5

Thus We have revealed it as a Lecture in Arabic, and have displayed therein certain threats, that peradventure they may keep from evil or that it may cause them to take heed.

S. XX, v. 113

Say: (It is) the truth from the Lord of you (all). Then whosoever will, let him believe, and whosoever will, let him disbelieve...

S.XVIII, v. 29

...Say they: He hath invented it? Nay, but they will not believe!

Then let them produce speech the like thereof, if they are truthful.

Or were they created out of naught? Or are they the creators?

Or did they create the heavens and the earth? Nay, but they are sure of nothing!

S. LII, vv. 33-36

Nay, I swear by the places of the stars—
And lo! that verily is a tremendous oath, if ye but knew—
That (this) is indeed a noble Quran
In a Book kept hidden
Which none toucheth save the purified,
A revelation from the Lord of the Worlds.
Is it this Statement that ye scorn,
And make denial thereof your livelihood?
Why, then, when (the soul) cometh up to the throat (of the dying)
And ye are at that moment looking
—And We are nearer unto him than ye are, but ye see not—
Why then, if ye are not in bondage (unto Us),
Do ye not force it back, if ye are truthful?

S. LVI, vv. 75-87

If We had caused this Quran to descend upon a mountain, Thou (O Muhammad) verily hadst seen it humbled, rent asunder by the fear of Allah. Such similitudes coin We for mankind that haply they may reflect.

S. LIX, v. 21

And We have made (this Scripture) easy in thy language only that they may heed.

S. XLIV, v. 58

A Guidance and a Mercy

And when thou bringest not a verse for them they say: Why hast thou not chosen it? Say: I follow only that which is inspired in me from my Lord. This (Quran) is insight from your Lord, and a guidance and a mercy for a people that believe.

S. VII, v. 203

And when the Quran is recited, give ear to it and pay heed, that ye may obtain mercy.

S. VII, v. 204

O mankind! There hath come unto you an exhortation from your Lord, a balm for that which is in the breasts, a guidance and a mercy for believers.

S. X, v. 57

Lo! this Quran guideth unto that which is straightest, and giveth tidings unto the believers who do good works that theirs will be a great reward.

S. XVII, v. 9

And We reveal of the Quran that which is a healing and a mercy for believers though it increase the evil-doers in naught save ruin.

S XVII, v. 82

A guidance and good tidings for believers
Who establish worship and pay the poor-due and are sure of the Hereafter.

S. XXVII, vv. 2,3

(This is) a Scripture that We have revealed unto thee, full of blessing, that they may ponder its revelations, and that men of understanding may reflect.

S. XXXVIII, v. 29

This is clear indication for mankind, and a guidance and a mercy for a folk whose faith is sure.

S. XLV, v. 20

When before it there was the Scripture of Moses, an example and a mercy; and this is a confirming Scripture in the Arabic language, that it may warn those who do wrong and bring good tidings for the righteous.

S. XLVI, v. 12

To those who Disbelieve

Those who disbelieve say: This is naught but a lie that he hath invented, and other folk have helped him with it, so that they have produced a slander and a lie.

And they say: Fables of the men of old which he hath had written down so that they are dictated to him morn and evening.

Say (unto them, O Muhammad): He Who knoweth the secret of the heavens and the earth hath revealed it. Lo! He ever is Forgiving, Merciful.

S. XXV, vv. 4-6

And the messenger saith: O my Lord! Lo! mine own folk make this Quran of no account.

Even so have We appointed unto every Prophet an opponent from among the guilty; but Allah sufficeth for a Guide and Helper.

And those who disbelive say: Why is the Quran not revealed unto him all at once? (It is revealed) thus that We may strengthen thy heart therewith; and We have arranged it in right order.

S. XXV, vv. 30-32

These are revelations of the Scripture that maketh plain.

It may be that thou tormentest thyself (O Muhammad) because they believe not.

If We will, We can send down on them from the sky a portent so that their necks would remain bowed before it.

Never cometh there unto them a fresh reminder from the Beneficent One, but they turn away from it.

Now they have denied (the Truth); but there will come unto them tidings of that whereat they used to scoff.

S. XXVI, vv. 2-6

...For those who believe it is a guidance and a healing; and as for those who disbelieve, there is a deafness in their ears, and it is blindness for them. Such are called to from afar.

S. XLI, v 44

But nay! I swear by all that ye see
And all that ye see not
That it is indeed the speech of an illustrious messenger.
It is not poet's speech—little is it that ye believe!
Nor diviner's speech—little is it that ye remember!
It is a revelation from the Lord of the Worlds.
And if he had invented false sayings concerning Us,
We assuredly had taken him by the right hand
And then severed his life-artery,

And not one of you could have held Us off from him.
And Lo! it is a warrant unto those who ward off (evil).
And Lo! We know that some among you will deny (it),
And Lo! it is indeed an anguish for the disbelievers.
And Lo! it is absolute truth.
So glorify the name of thy Tremendous Lord.

S. LXIX vv. 38-52

One of the greatest Portents

Nay, by the Moon
And the night when it withdraweth
And the dawn when it shineth forth,
Lo! this is one of the greatest (portents)
As a warning unto men,
Unto him of you who will advance or hang back.
Every soul is a pledge for its own deeds,

S. LXXIV, vv. 32-38

The Transcendent Majesty of Allah

Here are some of Allah's Sublime Attributes.

Say: He is Allah, the One!
Allah, the eternally Besought of all!
He begetteth not nor was begotten.
And there is none comparable unto Him.

S. CXII, vv. 1-4

Unto Allah belong the East and the West, and whither-soever ye turn, there is Allah's Countenance. Lo! Allah is All-Embracing, All-Knowing.

S. II. v. 115

Allah! There is no God save Him, the Alive, the Eternal. Neither slumber nor sleep overtaketh Him. Unto him belongeth whatsoever is in the heavens and whatsoever is in the earth. Who is he that intercedeth with Him save by His leave? He knoweth that which is in front of them and that which is behind them, while they encompass nothing of His knowledge save what He will. His throne includeth the heavens and the earth, and He is never weary of preserving them. He is the Sublime, the Tremendous.

S. II, v. 255

Vision comprehendeth Him not, but He comprehendeth (all) vision. He is the Subtile, Aware.

S. VI, v. 103

Unto Him belongeth whatsoever is in the heavens and whatsoever is in the earth, and whatsoever is between them, and whatsoever is beneath the sod.

And if thou speakest aloud, then lo! He knoweth the secret (thought) and (that which is yet) more hidden.

Allah! There is no God save Him. His are the most beautiful names.

S. XX. vv. 6-8

Allah is the Light of the heavens and the earth. The similitude of His Light is as a niche wherein is a lamp. The lamp is in a glass. The glass is as it were a shining star. (This lamp is) kindled from a blessed tree, an olive neither of the East nor of the West, whose oil would almost glow forth (of itself) though no fire touched it. Light upon light. Allah guideth unto His light whom He will. And Allah speaketh to mankind in allegories, for Allah is Knower of all things.

S. XXIV v. 35

And if all the trees were pens, and the sea, with seven more seas to help it, (were ink), the words of Allah could not be exhausted. Lo! Allah is Mighty, Wise.

Your creation and your raising (from the dead) are only as (the creation and the raising of) a single soul. Lo! Allah is Hearer, Knower!

S. XXXI, vv. 27,28

All that is in the heavens and the earth glorifieth Allah; and He is the Mighty, the Wise.

His is the Sovereignty of the heavens and the earth; He quickeneth and He giveth death; and He is Able to do all things.

He is the First and the Last, and the Outward and the Inward; and He is Knower of all things.

He it is Who created the heavens and the earth in six Days; then He mounted the Throne. He knoweth all that entereth the earth and all that emergeth therefrom and all that cometh down from the sky and all that ascendeth therein; and He is with you wheresoever ye may be. And Allah is Seer of what ye do.

His is the Sovereignty of the heavens and the earth, and unto Allah (all) things are brought back.

He causeth the night to pass into the day, and He causeth the day to pass into the night, and He is the Knower of all that is in the breasts.

S. LVII, vv. 1-6

He is Allah, than Whom there is no other God, the Knower of the Invisible and the Visible. He is the Beneficent, the Merciful.

He is Allah, than Whom there is no other God, the Sovereign Lord, the Holy One, Peace, the Keeper of Faith, the Guardian, the Majestic, the Compeller, the Superb. Glorified be Allah from all that they ascribe as partner (unto Him).

He is Allah, the Creator, the Shaper out of naught, the Fashioner. His are the most beautiful names. All that is in the heavens and the earth glorifieth Him, and He is the Mighty, the Wise.

S. LIX, vv. 22-24

THE PROPHET

Read: In the name of thy Lord Who createth,
Createth man from a clot.
Read: And thy Lord is the Most Bounteous,
Who teacheth by the pen,
Teacheth man that which he knew not.   s. XCVI, vv. 1-5

These are the words which the Prophet received in the vision at Hira.
They are the first of the Quran to be revealed.

We know well how their talk grieveth thee, though in
truth they deny not thee (Muhammad) but evil-doers flout
the revelations of Allah.

Messengers indeed have been denied before thee, and they
were patient under the denial and the persecution till Our
succour reached them. There is none to alter the decisions
of Allah. Already there hath reached thee (somewhat) of the
tidings of the messengers (We sent before).   s. VI, vv. 33, 34

Those who follow the messenger, the Prophet who can
neither read nor write, whom they will find described in the
Torah and the Gospel (which are) with them. He will enjoin
on them that which is right and forbid them that which is
wrong. He will make lawful for them all good things and
prohibit for them only the foul; and he will relieve them of
their burden and the fetters that they used to wear. Then
those who believe in him, and honour him, and help him, and
follow the light which is sent down with him: they are the
successful.

Say (O Muhammad): O mankind! Lo! I am the messenger
of Allah to you all—(the messenger of) Him unto whom
belongeth the Sovereignty of the heavens and the earth.
There is no God save Him. He quickeneth and He giveth
death. So believe in Allah and His messenger, the Prophet
who can neither read nor write, who believeth in Allah and
in His words and follow him that haply ye may be led aright.

S. VII, vv. 157, 158

Never cometh there unto them a new reminder from their Lord but they listen to it while they play,

With hearts preoccupied. And they confer in secret. The wrong-doers say: Is this other than a mortal like you? Will ye then succumb to magic when ye see (it)?

He saith: My Lord knoweth what is spoken in the heavens and the earth. He is the Hearer, the Knower.

Nay, say they, (these are but) muddled dreams; nay, he hath but invented it: nay, he is but a poet. Let him bring us a portent even as those of old (who were God's messengers) were sent (with portents).

S. XXI, vv. 2-5

Or say they: There is a madness in him? Nay, but he bringeth them the Truth; and most of them are haters of the Truth.

S. XXIII, v. 70

Lo! We have sent thee with the Truth, a bearer of glad tidings and a warner; and there is not a nation but a warner hath passed among them.

S. XXXV, v. 24

Say (unto them O Muhammad): I am only a mortal like you. It is inspired in me that your God is one God, therefor take the straight path unto Him and seek forgiveness of Him...

S. XLI, v. 6

But if they are averse, We have not sent thee as a warder over them. Thine is only to convey (the message)....

S. XLII, v. 48

And it is not (vouchsafed) to any mortal that Allah should speak to him unless (it be) by revelation or from behind a veil, or (that) He sendeth a messenger to reveal what He will by His leave. Lo! He is Exalted, Wise.

And thus have We inspired in thee (Muhammad) a Spirit of Our command. Thou knewest not what the Scripture was, nor what the Faith. But We have made it a light whereby We guide whom We will of Our bondmen. And lo! thou verily dost guide unto a right path.

The path of Allah, unto Whom belongeth whatsoever is in the heavens and whatsoever is in the earth. Do not all things reach Allah at last?

S. XLII, vv. 51-53

Say: I am no new thing among the messengers (of Allah),
nor know I what will be done with me or with you. I do but
follow that which is inspired in me, and I am but a plain
warner.

S. XLVI, v. 9

And when Jesus son of Mary said: O children of Israel!
Lo! I am the messenger of Allah unto you, confirming that
which was (revealed) before me in the Torah,[1] and bringing
good tidings of a messenger who cometh after me, whose
name is the Praised One.[2] Yet when he hath come unto them
with clear proofs, they say: This is mere magic.

S. LXI, v. 6

Even as We have sent unto you a messenger from among
you, who reciteth unto you Our revelations and causeth you
to grow, and teacheth you the Scripture and wisdom, and
teacheth you that which ye knew not.

Therefore remember Me, I will remember you. Give
thanks to Me, and reject not Me.

S. II, vv. 151, 152

By the morning hours
And by the night when it is stillest,
Thy Lord has not forsaken thee nor doth He hate thee,
And verily the latter portion will be better for thee than
the former,
And verily thy Lord will give unto thee so that thou
will be content.
Did He not find thee an orphan and protect (thee)?
Did He not find thee wandering and direct (thee)?
Did He not find thee destitute and enrich (thee)?
Therefor the orphan oppress not,
Therefor the beggar drive not away,
Therefor of the bounty of thy Lord be thy discourse.

S. XCIII, vv. 1-11

There was an interval, Pickthall writes, during which the Prophet
received no revelation and the idolaters mocked him, saying:
'Allah, of whom we used to hear so much, has forsaken poor Muhammad and now hates him.' Then came this revelation. The Prophet

---

1 Book of Moses.

2 Arabic—Ahmad. A name of the Prophet of Arabia. The promised comforter
was believed by many Christian communities of the East to be a Prophet yet to
come, and most of them accepted Muhammad as that Prophet.

had been a leading citizen of Mecca until he received his call. Now he was regarded as a madman. He was a man near fifty, and the prophecy in this Surah that 'the latter portion would be better for him than the former' must have seemed absurd to those who heard it. Yet the latter portion of the Prophet's life, the last ten years, is the most wonderful record of success in human history.

Solace

> Have We not caused thy bosom to dilate,
> And eased thee of the burden
> Which weighed down thy back;
> And exalted thy fame?
> But lo! with hardship goeth ease
> Lo! with hardship goeth ease;
> So when thou art relieved, still toil
> And strive to please thy Lord.

S. XCIV, vv. 1-8

According to Pickthall, this Surah was revealed 'at a time when the Prophet was derided and shunned after having been respected and courted...It refers to the inward assurance which the Prophet had received by revelation, and speaks of the future as accomplished, as is usual in the Quran, the revelation coming from a plane where time is not. Verse 4, speaking of his fame as exalted, must have seemed particularly absurd at that time of humiliation and persecution. But today, from every mosque in the world, the Prophet's name is cried, as that of the messenger of God, five times a day, and every Muslim prays for blessings on him when his name is mentioned.'

Succour

> When Allah's succour and the triumph cometh
> And thou seest mankind entering the religion of Allah in troops,
> Then hymn the praises of thy Lord, and seek forgiveness of Him. Lo! He is ever ready to show mercy.

S. CX, vv. 1-3

Pickthall writes that, according to tradition, this Surah was revealed at Mecca during the Prophet's farewell pilgrimage; it is considered to be 'the first announcement that the Prophet received of his approaching death.'

3

MAN

Creation of Man

He it is Who hath created you from clay, and hath decreed a term for you. A term is fixed with Him. Yet still ye doubt!

S. VI, v. 2

And We created you, then fashioned you, then told the angels: Fall ye prostrate before Adam! And they fell prostrate, all save Iblis, who was not of those who make prostration.

He said: What hindered thee that thou didst not fall prostrate when I bade thee? (Iblis) said: I am better than him. Thou createdst me of fire while him Thou didst create of mud.

He said: Then go down hence! It is not for thee to show pride here, so go forth! Lo! thou art of those degraded.

S.VII, vv. 11-13

Divine Spirit Breathed into Man

Then He fashioned him and breathed into him of His Spirit; and appointed for you hearing and sight and hearts. Small thanks give ye!

S. XXXII, v. 9

Man created of the best Stature

Surely We created man of the best stature
Then We reduced him to the lowest of the low,
Save those who believe and do good works, and theirs is a reward unfailing

S. XCV, vv. 4-6

Universe made subservient to Man

Allah is He Who created the heavens and the earth, and causeth water to descend from the sky, thereby producing fruits as food for you, and maketh the ships to be of service unto you, that they may run upon the sea at His command, and hath made of service unto you the rivers;

And maketh the sun and the moon, constant in their courses, to be of service unto you, and hath made of service unto you the night and the day.

And he giveth you all ye ask of Him, and if ye would count the bounty of Allah ye cannot reckon it. Lo! man is verily a wrong-doer, an ingrate.

S. XIV, vv. 32-34

And He hath constrained the night and the day and the sun and the moon to be of service unto you, and the stars are made subservient by His command. Lo! herein indeed are portents for people who have sense.

And whatsoever He hath created for you in the earth of divers hues, lo! therein is indeed a portent for people who take heed.

And He it is Who hath constrained the sea to be of service that ye eat fresh meat from thence, and bring forth from thence ornaments which ye wear. And thou seest the ships ploughing it that ye (mankind) may seek of His bounty, and that haply ye may give thanks.

And He hath cast into the earth firm hills that it quake not with you, and streams and roads that ye may find a way.

And landmarks (too), and by the star they find a way.

S. XVI, vv. 12-16

And hath made of service unto you whatsoever is in the heavens and whatsoever is in the earth; it is all from Him. Lo! herein verily are portents for a people who reflect.

S. XLV, v. 13

Man is ungrateful

And We have given you (mankind) power in the earth, and appointed for you therein livelihoods. Little give ye thanks!

S. VII, v. 10

Man tireth not of praying for good, and if ill toucheth him, then he is disheartened, desperate.

When We show favour unto man, he withdraweth and turneth aside, but when ill toucheth him then he aboundeth in prayer.

S. XLI, vv. 49, 51

Man has become unfaithful to the Trust

Lo! We offered the trust unto the heavens and the earth and the hills, but they shrank from bearing it and were afraid of it. And man assumed it. Lo! he hath proved a tyrant and a fool.

S. XXXIII, v. 72

4

THE BELIEVERS

A True Believer

Say: Come, I will recite unto you that which your Lord
hath made a sacred duty for you: that ye ascribe no thing
as partner unto Him and that ye do good to parents, and
that ye slay not your children because of penury—We provide
for you and for them—and that ye draw not nigh to lewd
things whether open or concealed. And that ye slay not
the life which Allah hath made sacred, save in the course
of justice. This He hath commanded you, in order that ye
may discern.

And approach not the wealth of the orphan save with that
which is better, till he reach maturity. Give full measure
and full weight, in justice. We task not any soul beyond
its scope. And if ye give your word, do justice thereunto,
even though it be (against) a kinsman; and fulfil the covenant
of Allah. This He commandeth you that haply ye may
remember.

S. VI, vv. 151, 152

(Triumphant) are those who turn repentant (to Allah),
those who serve (Him), those who praise (Him), those who
fast, those who bow down, those who fall prostrate (in
worship), those who enjoin the right and who forbid the
wrong and those who keep the limits (ordained) of Allah—
And give glad tidings to believers!

S. IX, v. 112

Lo! men who surrender unto Allah, and women who
surrender, and men who believe and women who believe,
and men who obey and women who obey, and men who
speak the truth and women who speak the truth, and men
who persevere (in righteousness) and women who persevere,
and men who are humble and women who are humble, and
men who give alms and women who give alms, and men
who fast and women who fast, and men who guard their
modesty and women who guard (their modesty), and men

who remember Allah much and women who remember—
Allah hath prepared for them forgiveness and a vast reward.

S. XXXIII, v. 35

To Those Who Believe

...Allah loveth those who put their trust (in Him).

S. III, v. 159

As for those who believe in Allah, and hold fast unto
Him, them He will cause to enter into His mercy and grace,
and will guide them unto Him by a straight road.

S. IV, v. 175

...If ye establish worship and pay the poor-due, and
believe in My messengers and support them, and lend unto
Allah a kindly loan,[1] surely I shall remit your sins, and
surely I shall bring you into Gardens underneath which
rivers flow. Whoso among you disbelieveth after this will
go astray from a plain road.

S. V, v. 12

O ye who believe! Whoso of you becometh a renegade
from his religion, (know that in his stead) Allah will bring
a people whom He loveth and who love Him, humble toward
believers, stern toward disbelievers, striving in the way of
Allah, and fearing not the blame of any blamer. Such is the
grace of Allah which He giveth unto whom He will. Allah
is All-Embracing, All-Knowing.

S. V, v. 54

If only the People of the Scripture would believe and ward
off (evil), surely We should remit their sins from them and
surely We should bring them into Gardens of Delight.

S. V, v. 65

Lo! those who believe (in that which is revealed unto thee,
Muhammad), and those who are Jews, and Christians, and
Sabaeans—whoever believeth in Allah and the Last Day and
doeth right—surely their reward is with their Lord, and there
shall no fear come upon them neither shall they grieve.

S. II, v. 62

Those who believe and obscure not their belief by wrong-
doing, theirs is safety; and they are rightly guided.

S. VI, v. 82

1 A loan without interest or thought of gain.

They only are the (true) believers whose hearts feel fear when Allah is mentioned, and when His revelations are recited unto them they increase their faith, and who trust in their Lord;

Who establish worship and spend of that We have bestowed on them.

Those are they who are in truth believers. For them are grades (of honour) with their Lord, and pardon, and a bountiful provision.

S. VIII, vv. 2-4

And the believers, men and women, are protecting friends one of another; they enjoin the right and forbid the wrong, and they establish worship and they pay the poor-due, and they obey Allah and His messenger. As for these, Allah will have mercy on them. Lo! Allah is Mighty, Wise.

S. IX, v. 71

Lo! verily the friends of Allah are (those) on whom fear (cometh) not, nor do they grieve.

Those who believe and keep their duty (to Allah),

Theirs are good tidings in the life of the world and in the Hereafter—There is no changing the Words of Allah—that is the Supreme Triumph.

S. X, vv. 62-64

Successful indeed are the believers
Who are humble in their prayers,
And who shun vain conversation,
And who are payers of the poor-due;
And who guard their modesty—

S. XXIII, vv. 1-5

And who are shepherds of their pledge and their covenant,
And who pay heed to their prayers.
These are the heirs
Who will inherit Paradise. There they will abide.

S. XXIII, vv. 8-11

Do men imagine that they will be left (at ease) because they say, We believe, and will not be tested with affliction?

S. XXIX, v. 2

As for those who strive in Us, We surely guide them to Our paths, and lo! Allah is with the good.

S. XXIX, v. 69

And whoso bringeth the truth and believeth therein—Such are the dutiful.

They shall have what they will of their Lord's bounty. That is the reward of the good:

That Allah will remit from them the worst of what they did, and will pay them for reward the best they used to do.

S. XXXIX, vv. 33-35

The believers are naught else than brothers. Therefore make peace between your brethren and observe your duty to Allah that haply ye may obtain mercy.

S. XLIX, v. 10

5

THE RIGHTEOUS

Pickthall in his note on Surah II writes:

All through the Surah (II) runs the note of warning, which sounds indeed throughout the whole Koran, that it is not the mere profession of a creed, but righteous conduct, which is true religion. There is the repeated announcement that the religion of Abraham, to which Judaism and Christianity (which springs from Judaism) trace their origin, is the only true religion, and that that religion consists in the surrender of man's will and purpose to the Will and Purpose of the Lord of Creation as manifested in His Creation and revealed by way of guidance through successive Prophets. Of sincerity in that religion the one test is conduct and the standard of that religion is for all alike.

Righteousness

It is not righteousness that ye turn your faces to the East and the West; but righteous is he who believeth in Allah and the Last Day and the angels and the Scripture and the Prophets; and giveth wealth, for love of Him, to kinsfolk and to orphans and the needy and the wayfarer and to those who ask, and to set slaves free; and observeth proper worship and payeth the poor-due. And those who keep their treaty when they make one, and the patient in tribulation and adversity and time of stress. Such are they who are sincere. Such are the God-fearing.

S. II, v. 177

The (faithful) slaves of the Beneficent are they who walk the earth modestly, and when the foolish ones address them answer: Peace;

And who spend the night before their Lord, prostrate and standing,

And who say: Our Lord! Avert from us the doom of hell; lo! the doom thereof is anguish;

Lo! it is wretched as abode and station;

And those who, when they spend, are neither prodigal nor grudging; and there is ever a firm station between the two;

And those who cry not unto any other god along with Allah, nor take the life which Allah hath forbidden save in (course of) justice, nor commit adultery—and whoso doeth this shall pay the penalty;

The doom will be doubled for him on the Day òf Resurrection, and he will abide therein disdained for ever;

Save him who repenteth and believeth and doth righteous work; as for such, Allah will change their evil deeds to good deeds. Allah is ever Forgiving, Merciful.

And whosoever repenteth and doeth good, he verily repenteth toward Allah with true repentance—

And those who will not witness vanity, but when they pass near senseless play, pass by with dignity.

And those who, when they are reminded of the revelations of their Lord, fall not deaf and blind thereat.

And who say: Our Lord! Vouchsafe us comfort of our wives and of our offspring, and make us patterns for (all) those who ward off (evil).

They will be awarded the high place forasmuch as they were steadfast, and they will meet therein with welcome and the word of peace,

Abiding there for ever. Happy is it as abode and station!

S. XXV, vv. 63-76

Such as keep the pact of Allah, and break not the covenant;

Such as unite that which Allah hath commanded should be joined, and fear their Lord, and dread a woeful reckoning;

Such as persevere in seeking their Lord's Countenance and are regular in prayer and spend of that which We bestow upon them secretly and openly, and overcome evil with good. Theirs will be the sequel of the (heavenly) Home,

Gardens of Eden which they enter, along with all who do right of their fathers and their helpmeets and their seed. The angels enter unto them from every gate,

(Saying): Peace be unto you because ye persevered. Ah, passing sweet will be the sequel of the (heavenly) Home.

S. XIII, vv. 20-24

Who are constant at their worship
And in whose wealth there is a right acknowledged
For the beggar and the destitute;
And those who believe in the Day of Judgment;
And those who are fearful of their Lord's doom—
Lo! the doom of their Lord is that before which none can feel secure—
And those who preserve their chastity
Save with their wives and those whom their right hands possess, for thus they are not blameworthy;
But whoso seeketh more than that, those are they who are transgressors;
And those who keep their pledges and their covenant;
And those who stand by their testimony
And those who are attentive at their worship,
These will dwell in Gardens, honoured.

S. LXX, vv. 23-35

Ah, what will convey unto thee what the Ascent is!—
(It is) to free a slave,
And to feed in the day of hunger
An orphan near of kin,
Or some poor wretch in misery,
And to be of those who believe and exhort one another to perseverance and exhort one another to pity.
Their place will be on the right hand.
But those who disbelieve Our revelations, their place will be on the left hand.
Fire will be an awning over them.

S. XC, vv. 12-20

They believe in Allah and the Last Day, and enjoin right conduct and forbid indecency, and vie one with another in good works. They are of the righteous.

S. III, v. 114

Your Lord is Best Aware of what is in your minds. If ye are righteous, then lo! He was ever Forgiving unto those who turn (unto Him).

S. XVII, v. 25

And verily We have written in the Scripture, after the Reminder: My righteous slaves will inherit the earth.

S. XXI, v. 105

And they are ordered naught else than to serve Allah, keeping religion pure for Him, as men by nature upright, and to establish worship and to pay the poor-due. That is true religion.

S. XCVIII, v. 5

Those who Believe and do Good Works

...give glad tidings (O Muhammad) unto those who believe and do good works; that theirs are Gardens underneath which rivers flow...

S. II, v. 25

Establish worship, pay the poor-due, and bow your heads with those who bow (in worship).

S. II, v. 43

...whoever believeth in Allah and the Last Day and doeth right—surely their reward is with their Lord, and there shall no fear come upon them neither shall they grieve.

S. II, v. 62

And those who believe and do good works; such are rightful owners of the Garden. They will abide therein.

S. II, v. 82

Establish worship and pay the poor-due; and whatever of good ye send before (you) for your souls, ye will find it with Allah. Lo! Allah is Seer of what ye do.

S. II, v. 110

...believe in Allah and His messengers. If ye believe and ward off (evil), yours will be a vast reward.

S. III, v. 179

And as for those who believe and do good works, We shall make them enter Gardens underneath which rivers flow —to dwell therein for ever...

S. IV, v. 57

But as for those who believe and do good works We shall bring them into Gardens underneath which rivers flow, wherein they will abide for ever...

S. IV, v. 122

And whoso doeth good works, whether of male or female, and he (or she) is a believer, such will enter paradise and they will not be wronged the dint in a date-stone.

S. IV, v. 124

Then, as for those who believed and did good works, unto them will He pay their wages in full, adding unto them of His bounty; and as for those who were scornful and proud, them will He punish with a painful doom. And they will not find for them, against Allah, any protecting friend or helper.

S. IV, v. 173

Allah hath promised those who believe and do good works: Theirs will be forgiveness and immense reward.

S. V, v. 9

...be mindful of your duty (to Allah), and believe, and do good works; and again: be mindful of your duty, and believe; and once again: be mindful of your duty, and do right. Allah loveth the good.

S. V, v. 93

We send not the messengers save as bearers of good news and warners. Whoso believeth and doeth right, there shall no fear come upon them neither shall they grieve.

S. VI, v. 48

But (as for) those who believe and do good works—We tax not any soul beyond its scope—Such are rightful owners of the Garden. They abide therein.

S. VII, v. 42

O ye who believe! If ye keep your duty to Allah, He will give you discrimination (between right and wrong) and will rid you of your evil thoughts and deeds, and will forgive you. Allah is of Infinite Bounty.

S. VIII, v. 29

Unto Him is the return of all of you; it is a promise of Allah in truth. Lo! He produceth creation, then reproduceth it, that He may reward those who believe and do good works with equity; while, as for those who disbelieve, theirs will be a boiling drink and painful doom because they disbelieved.

S. X, v. 4

Lo! those who believe and do good works and humble themselves before their Lord: such are rightful owners of the Garden; they will abide therein.

S. XI, v. 23

Those who believe and do right: Joy is for them, and bliss (their) journey's end.

S. XIII, v. 29

And those who believed and did good works are made to enter Gardens underneath which rivers flow, therein abiding by permission of their Lord, their greeting therein: Peace!

S. XIV, v. 23

Whosoever doeth right, whether male or female, and is a believer, him verily We shall quicken with good life, and We shall pay them a recompense in proportion to the best of what they used to do.

S. XVI, v. 97

Lo! Allah is with those who keep their duty unto Him and those who are doers of good.

S. XVI, v. 128

And whoso desireth the Hereafter and striveth for it with the effort necessary, being a believer; for such, their effort findeth favour (with their Lord).

S. XVII, v. 19

Lo! those who believe and do good works, the Beneficent will appoint for them love.

S. XIX, v. 96

But whoso cometh unto Him a believer, having done good works, for such are the high stations.

S. XX, v. 75

...him who repenteth and believeth and doth righteous works; as for such, Allah will change their evil deeds to good deeds. Allah is ever Forgiving, Merciful.

S. XXV, v. 70

But as for him who shall repent and believe and do right, he haply may be one of the successful (on that day).

S. XXVIII, v. 67

And as for those who believe and do good works, We shall remit from them their evil deeds and shall repay them the best that they did.

S. XXIX, v. 7

And as for those who believe and do good works, We verily shall make them enter in among the righteous.

S. XXIX, v. 9

Those who believe and do good works, them verily We shall house in lofty dwellings of the Garden underneath which rivers flow. There they will dwell secure. How sweet the guerdon of the toilers,
Who persevere, and put their trust in their Lord!

S. XXIX, vv. 58, 59

Those who establish worship and pay the poor-due and have sure faith in the Hereafter.
Such have guidance from their Lord. Such are the successful.

S. XXXI, vv. 4, 5

But as for those who believe and do good works, for them are Gardens of Retreat—a welcome (in reward) for what they used to do.

S. XXXII, v. 19

That He may reward those who believe and do good works. For them is pardon and a rich provision.

S. XXXIV, v. 4

...those who believe and do good works, theirs will be forgiveness and a great reward.

S. XXXV, v. 7

Whoso doeth an ill-deed, he will be repaid the like thereof, while whoso doeth right, whether male or female, and is a believer, (all) such will enter the Garden, where they will be nourished without stint.

S. XL, v. 40

Lo! as for those who believe and do good works, for them is a reward enduring.

S. XLI, v. 8

Thou seest the wrong-doers fearful of that which they have earned, and it will surely befall them; while those who believe and do good works (will be) in flowering meadows of the Gardens, having what they wish from their Lord. This is the great preferment.
This it is which Allah announceth unto His bondmen who believe and do good works. Say (O Muhammad, unto mankind): I ask of you no fee therefor, save lovingkindness among kinsfolk. And whoso scoreth a good deed We add unto its good for him. Lo! Allah is Forgiving, Responsive.

S. XLII, vv. 22, 23

Then, as for those who believed and did good works, their Lord will bring them in unto His mercy. That is the evident triumph.

S. XLV, v. 30

And those who believe and do good works and believe in that which is revealed unto Muhammad—and it is the truth from their Lord—He riddeth them of their ill-deeds and improveth their state.

S. XLVII, v. 2

Lo! Allah will cause those who believe and do good works to enter Gardens underneath which rivers flow; while those who disbelieve take their comfort in this life and eat even as the cattle eat, and the Fire is their habitation.

S. XLVII, v. 12

...Allah hath promised, unto such of them as believe and do good works, forgiveness and immense reward.

S. XLVIII, v. 29

Ye should believe in Allah and his messenger, and should strive for the cause of Allah with your wealth and your lives. That is better for you, if ye did but know.

He will forgive you your sins and bring you into Gardens underneath which rivers flow, and pleasant dwellings in Gardens of Eden. That is the supreme triumph.

S. LXI, vv. 11, 12

A messenger reciting unto you the revelations of Allah made plain, that He may bring forth those who believe and do good works from darkness unto light. And whosoever believeth in Allah and doeth right, He will bring him into Gardens underneath which rivers flow, therein to abide for ever. Allah hath made good provision for him.

S. LXV, v. 11

...those who believe and do good works, theirs is a reward unfailing.

S. XCV, v. 6

...lo! those who believe and do good works are the best of created beings.

Their reward is with their Lord: Gardens of Eden underneath which rivers flow, wherein they dwell for ever. Allah hath pleasure in them and they have pleasure in Him. This is (in store) for him who feareth his Lord.

S. XCVIII, vv. 7, 8

Importance of Good Deeds

The following verses emphasise further the importance of good deeds:

...Lo! the noblest of you, in the sight of Allah, is the best in conduct...

S. XLIX, v. 13

...Allah loveth those whose deeds are good.

S. III, v. 148

The steadfast, and the truthful, and the obedient, those who spend (and hoard not), those who pray for pardon in the watches of the night.

S. III, v. 17

And whatever good they do, they will not be denied the meed thereof. Allah is Aware of those who ward off (evil).

S. III, v. 115

Those who spend (of that which Allah hath given them) in ease and in adversity, those who control their wrath and are forgiving toward mankind; Allah loveth the good;

S. III, v. 134

Lo! Allah wrongeth not even of the weight of an ant; and if there is a good deed, He will double it and will give (the doer) from His presence an immense reward.

S. IV, v. 40

If ye do good openly or keep it secret, or forgive evil, lo! Allah is ever Forgiving, Powerful.

S. IV, v. 149

For those who do good is the best (reward) and more (thereto). Neither dust nor ignominy cometh near their faces. Such are rightful owners of the Garden; they will abide therein.

S. X, v. 26

Allah increaseth in right guidance those who walk aright, and the good deeds which endure are better in thy Lord's sight for reward, and better for resort.

S. XIX v. 76

Whosoever surrendereth his purpose to Allah while doing good, he verily hath grasped the firm hand-hold. Unto Allah belongeth the sequel of all things.

S. XXXI, v. 22

And Allah delivereth those who ward off (evil) because of their deserts. Evil toucheth them not, nor do they grieve.

S. XXXIX, v. 61

Lo! Those who say: Our Lord is Allah, and afterward are upright, the angels descend upon them, saying: Fear not, nor grieve, but hear good tidings of the paradise which ye are promised.

We are your protecting friends in the life of the world and in the Hereafter. There ye will have (all) that your souls desire, and there ye will have (all) for which ye pray.

A gift of welcome from the Forgiving, the Merciful.

S. XLI, vv. 30-32

Lo! those who say: Our Lord is Allah, and thereafter walk aright, there shall no fear come upon them neither shall they grieve.

Such are rightful owners of the Garden, immortal therein, as a reward for what they used to do.

S. XLVI, vv. 13, 14

While as for those who walk aright, He addeth to their guidance, and giveth them their protection (against evil).

S. XLVII, v. 17

Lo! those who keep from evil will dwell amid gardens and watersprings,

Taking that which their Lord giveth them; for lo! aforetime they were doers of good;

They used to sleep but little of the night,

And ere the dawning of each day would seek forgiveness,

And in their wealth the beggar and the outcast had due share.

S. LI, vv. 15-19

So keep your duty to Allah as best ye can, and listen, and obey, and spend; that is better for your souls. And whoso is saved from his own greed, such are the successful.

S. LXIV, v. 16

Lo! those who fear their lord in secret, theirs will be forgiveness and a great reward.

S. LXVII, v. 12

6

PRAYER

We verily created man and We know what his soul whispereth to him, and We are nearer to him than his jugular vein.

S. L, v. 16

Be guardians of your prayers,[1] and of the midmost prayer, and stand up with devotion to Allah.

S. II, v. 238

When ye have performed the act of worship, remember Allah, standing, sitting and reclining. And when ye are in safety, observe proper worship. Worship at fixed times hath been enjoined on the believers.

S. IV, v. 103

And do thou (O Muhammad) remember thy Lord within thyself humbly and with awe, below thy breath, at morn and evening. And be not thou of the neglectful.

S. VII, v. 205

Establish worship at the two ends of the day and in some watches of the night. Lo! good deeds annul ill-deeds. This is a reminder for the mindful.

S. XI, v. 114

Establish worship at the going down of the sun until the dark of night, and (the recital of) the Quran at dawn. Lo! (the recital of) the Quran at dawn is ever witnessed.

And some part of the night awake for it, a largess for thee. It may be that thy Lord will raise thee to a praised estate.

S. XVII, vv. 78, 79

Remember the name of thy Lord at morn and evening.

And worship Him (a portion) of the night. And glorify Him through the livelong night.

S. LXXVI, vv. 25, 26

O ye who believe! Remember Allah with much remembrance.

And glorify Him early and late.

S. XXXIII, vv. 41, 42

---

[1] The four pillars of Faith are: Prayer, Zakat (the poor-due), Pilgrimage, Fasting.

Then have patience (O Muhammad). Lo! the promise of Allah is true. And ask forgiveness of thy sin, and hymn the praise of thy Lord at fall of night and in the early hours.

S. XL, v. 55

...hymn the praise of thy Lord when thou uprisest,
And in the night-time also hymn His praise, and at the setting of the stars.

S. LII, vv. 48, 49

Say: Lo! my worship and my sacrifice and my living and my dying are for Allah, Lord of the Worlds.

S. VI, v. 162

And put thy trust in the Mighty, the Merciful.
Who seeth thee when thou standest up (to pray)
And (seeth) thine abasement among those who fall prostrate (in worship).

S. XXVI, vv. 217-219

Recite that which hath been inspired in thee of the Scripture, and establish worship. Lo! worship preserveth from lewdness and iniquity, but verily remembrance of Allah is more important. And Allah knoweth what ye do.

S. XXIX, v. 45

Is he who payeth adoration in the watches of the night, prostrate and standing, bewaring of the Hereafter and hoping for the mercy of his Lord, (to be accounted equal with a disbeliever)? Say (unto them, O Muhammad): Are those who know equal with those who know not? But only men of understanding will pay heed.

S. XXXIX, v. 9

...So recite of it (Quran) that which is easy (for you), and establish worship and pay the poor-due, and (so) lend unto Allah a goodly loan. Whatsoever good ye send before you for your souls, ye will find it with Allah, better and greater in the recompense. And seek forgiveness of Allah. Lo! Allah is Forgiving, Merciful.

S. LXXIII, v. 20

Invoking Allah's Help

...I answer the prayer of the suppliant when he crieth unto Me. So let them hear My call and let them trust in Me, in order that they may be led aright.

S. II, v. 186

Our Lord! Forgive me and my parents and believers on the day when the account is cast.

S. XIV, v. 41

And say: My Lord! Cause me to come in with a firm incoming and to go out with a firm outgoing. And give me from Thy presence a sustaining Power.

S. XVII, v. 80

And your Lord hath said: Pray unto Me and I will hear your prayer...

S. XL, v. 60

7

THE STEADFAST

O ye who believe! Seek help in steadfastness and prayer. Lo! Allah is with the steadfast.

S. II, v. 153

And surely We shall try you with something of fear and hunger, and loss of wealth and lives and crops; but give glad tidings to the steadfast,

Who say, when a misfortune striketh them: Lo! we are Allah's and lo! unto Him we are returning.

Such are they on whom are blessings from their Lord, and mercy. Such are the rightly guided.

S. II, vv. 155-157

...if ye persevere (in faith) and ward off (evil), then that is of the steadfast heart of things.

S. III, v. 186

And obey Allah and His messenger, and dispute not one with another lest ye falter and your strength depart from you; but be steadfast! Lo! Allah is with the steadfast.

S. VIII, v. 46

That which ye have wasteth away, and that which Allah hath remaineth. And verily We shall pay those who are steadfast a recompense in proportion to the best of what they used to do.

S. XVI, v. 96

And whosoever striveth, striveth only for himself, for lo! Allah is altogether Independent of (His) creatures.

S. XXIX, v. 6

...Establish worship and enjoin kindness and forbid iniquity, and persevere whatever may befall thee. Lo! that is of the steadfast heart of things.

S. XXXI, v. 17

Say: O My bondmen who believe! Observe your duty to your Lord. For those who do good in this world there is good, and Allah's earth is spacious. Verily the steadfast will be paid their wages without stint.

S. XXXIX, v. 10

And verily We shall try you till We know those of you who strive hard (for the cause of Allah) and the steadfast, and till We test your record.

S. XLVII, v. 31

Lo! with hardship goeth ease;
So when thou art relieved, still toil
And strive to please thy Lord.

S. XCIV, vv. 6-8

Patience

Seek help in patience and prayer; and truly it is hard save for the humble-minded,
Who know that they will have to meet their Lord, and that unto Him they are returning.

S. II, vv. 45, 46

And have patience, (O Muhammad), for lo! Allah loseth not the wages of the good.

S. XI, v. 115

...give good tidings (O Muhammad) to...the patient of whatever may befall them...

S. XXII, vv. 34-35

Lord of the East and the West; there is no God save Him; so choose thou Him alone for thy defender.
And bear with patience what they utter, and part from them with a fair leave-taking.

S. LXXIII, vv. 9, 10

For the sake of thy Lord, be patient!

S. LXXIV, v. 7

Endurance

O ye who believe! Endure, outdo all others in endurance, be ready, and observe your duty to Allah, in order that ye may succeed.

S. III, v. 200

If ye punish, then punish with the like of that wherewith ye were afflicted. But if ye endure patiently, verily it is better for the patient.
Endure thou patiently (O Muhammad). Thine endurance is only by (the help of) Allah. Grieve not for them, and be not in distress because of that which they devise.
Lo! Allah is with those who keep their duty unto Him and those who are doers of good.

S. XVI, vv. 126-128

By the declining day,
Lo! man is in a state of loss,
Save those who believe and do good works, and exhort
one another to truth and exhort one another to endurance.

S. CIII, vv. 1-3

8

KINDNESS

A kind word with forgiveness is better than almsgiving followed by injury...

S. II, v. 263

And serve Allah. Ascribe no thing as partner unto Him. (Show) kindness unto parents, and unto near kindred, and orphans, and the needy, and unto the neighbour who is of kin (unto you) and the neighbour who is not of kin, and the fellow-traveller[1] and the wayfarer and (the slaves) whom your right hands possess...

S. IV, v. 36

Keep to forgiveness (O Muhammad), and enjoin kindness, and turn away from the ignorant.

S. VII, v. 199

Lo! Allah enjoineth justice and kindness, and giving to kinsfolk, and forbiddeth lewdness and abomination and wickedness. He exhorteth you in order that ye may take heed.[2]

S. XVI, v. 90

...enjoin kindness and forbid iniquity...

S. XXXI, v. 17

This it is which Allah announceth unto His bondmen who believe and do good works. Say (O Muhammad, unto mankind): I ask of you no fee therefor, save lovingkindness among kinsfolk...

S. XLII, v. 23

Small Kindnesses

Hast thou observed him who belieth religion?
That is he who repelleth the orphan,
And urgeth not the feeding of the needy.
Ah, woe unto worshippers
Who are heedless of their prayer;

---

[1] Arberry translates the relevant phrase as 'the companion at your side'.
[2] Since the time of Omar II the Omayyad, this verse has been recited at the end of every weekly sermon in all Sunni congregations.

Who would be seen (at worship)
Yet refuse small kindnesses!

S. CVII, vv. 1-7

Kindness to Parents

...Worship none save Allah (only), and be good to parents and to kindred and to orphans and the needy, and speak kindly to mankind; and establish worship and pay the poor-due...

S. II, v. 83

It is prescribed for you, when death approacheth one of you, if he leave wealth, that he bequeath unto parents and near relatives in kindness. (This is) a duty for all those who ward off (evil).

S. II, v. 180

Say: Come I will recite unto you that which your Lord hath made a sacred duty for you...that ye do good to parents...

S. VI, v. 151

Thy Lord hath decreed, that ye worship none save Him, and (that ye show) kindness to parents. If one of them or both of them attain old age with thee, say not 'Fie' unto them nor repulse them, but speak unto them a gracious word.

And lower unto them the wing of submission through mercy, and say: My Lord! Have mercy on them both as they did care for me when I was little.

S. XVII, vv. 23, 24

We have enjoined on man kindness to parents; but if they strive to make thee join with Me that of which thou hast no knowledge, then obey them not...

S. XXIX, v. 8

And We have enjoined upon man concerning his parents—His mother beareth him in weakness upon weakness, and his weaning is in two years—Give thanks unto Me and unto thy parents. Unto Me is the journeying.

But if they strive with thee to make thee ascribe unto Me as partner that of which thou hast no knowledge, then obey them not. Consort with them in the world kindly, and follow the path of him who repenteth unto Me...

S. XXXI, vv. 14, 15

And We have commended unto man kindness toward parents...

S. XLVI, v. 15

We may here recall that the Prophet has said: Paradise lies at the feet of the mother.

Kindness to Women

There are many verses in the Quran relating to the rights of women. As Pickthall sums up in his Introduction: With the Quran as his support and guide, the Prophet 'raised woman from the status of a chattel to complete legal equality with man'. Here only a few verses bearing on the treatment of women have been cited:

...Lo! I suffer not the work of any worker, male or female, to be lost. Ye proceed one from another...

S. III, v. 195

Pickthall notes: The expression 'Ye proceed one from another' which recurs in the Quran is a reminder to men that women are of the same human status as themselves.

When ye have divorced women, and they have reached their term[1] then retain them in kindness or release them in kindness. Retain them not to their hurt so that you transgress (the limits). He who doeth that hath wronged his soul...

S. II, v. 231

For divorced women a provision in kindness: a duty for those who ward off (evil).

S. II, v. 241

O ye who believe! It is not lawful for you to...put constraint upon them (women) that ye may take away a part of that which ye have given them, unless they be guilty of flagrant lewdness. But consort with them in kindness, for if ye hate them it may happen that ye hate a thing wherein Allah hath placed much good.

And if ye wish to exchange one wife for another and ye have given unto one of them a sum of money (however great), take nothing from it. Would ye take it by the way of calumny and open wrong?

S. IV, vv. 19, 20

[1] Three monthly courses.

Covet not the thing in which Allah hath made some of you to excel others. Unto men a fortune from that which they have earned, and unto women a fortune from that which they have earned...

S. IV, v. 32

And of His signs is this: He created for you helpmeets from yourselves that ye might find rest in them, and He ordained between you love and mercy. Lo! herein indeed are portents for folk who reflect.

S. XXX, v. 21

9

SPENDING IN THE WAY OF ALLAH

Spend your wealth for the cause of Allah, and be not cast by your own hands to ruin; and do good. Lo! Allah loveth the beneficent.

S. II, v. 195

...That which ye spend for good (must go) to parents and near kindred and orphans and the needy and the wayfarer. And whatsoever good ye do, lo! Allah is Aware of it.

S. II, v. 215

...And they ask thee what they ought to spend. Say: That which is superfluous...

S. II, v. 219

Those who spend their wealth by night and day, by stealth and openly, verily their reward is with their Lord, and there shall no fear come upon them neither shall they grieve.

S. II, v. 274

Ye will not attain unto piety until ye spend of that which ye love. And whatsoever ye spend, Allah is Aware thereof.

S. III, v. 92

Who hoard their wealth and enjoin avarice on others, and hide that which Allah hath bestowed upon them of His bounty. For disbelievers We prepare a shameful doom;

And (also) those who spend their wealth in order to be seen of men, and believe not in Allah nor the Last Day. Whoso taketh Satan for a comrade, a bad comrade hath he.

What have they (to fear) if they believe in Allah and the Last Day and spend (aright) of that which Allah hath bestowed upon them, when Allah is ever Aware of them (and all they do)?

S. IV, vv. 37-39

Tell My bondmen who believe to establish worship and spend of that which We have given them, secretly and publicly, before a day cometh wherein there will be neither traffick nor befriending.

S. XIV, v. 31

Give the kinsman his due, and the needy, and the way-farer, and squander not (thy wealth) in wantonness.

S. XVII, v. 26

So give to the kinsman his due, and to the needy, and to the wayfarer. That is best for those who seek Allah's Count-enance. And such are they who are successful.

S. XXX, v. 38

So keep your duty to Allah as best ye can, and listen, and obey, and spend; that is better for your souls. And whoso is saved from his own greed, such are the successful.

If ye lend unto Allah a goodly loan, He will double it for you and will forgive you, for Allah is Responsive, Clement.

S. LXIV, vv. 16, 17

Almsgiving

Those who spend their wealth for the cause of Allah and afterward make not reproach and injury to follow that which they have spent; their reward is with their Lord, and there shall no fear come upon them, neither shall they grieve.

A kind word with forgiveness is better than almsgiving followed by injury...

O ye who believe! Render not vain your almsgiving by reproach and injury, like him who spendeth his wealth only to be seen of men and believeth not in Allah and the Last Day...

S. II, vv. 262-264

If ye publish your almsgiving, it is well, but if ye hide it and give it to the poor, it will be better for you, and will atone for some of your ill-deeds. Allah is Informed of what ye do.

S. II, v. 271

...who enjoineth almsgiving and kindness and peace-making among the people. Whoso doeth that, seeking the good pleasure of Allah, We shall bestow on him a vast reward.

S. IV, v. 114

...that which ye give in charity, seeking Allah's Count-enance, hath increase manifold.

S. XXX, v. 39

Lo! those who give alms, both men and women, and lend unto Allah a goodly loan, it will be doubled for them, and theirs will be a rich reward.

S. LVII, v. 18

And feed with food the needy wretch, the orphan and the prisoner, for love of Him,

(Saying): We feed you, for the sake of Allah only. We wish for no reward nor thanks from you;

Lo! we fear from our Lord a day of frowning and of fate.

S. LXXVI, vv. 8-10

As for him who giveth and is dutiful (toward Allah)
And believeth in goodness;
Surely We will ease his way unto the state of ease.

S. XCII, vv. 5-7

Who giveth his wealth that he may grow (in goodness),
And none hath with him any favour for reward,
Except as seeking (to fulfil) the purpose of his Lord Most High.
He verily will be content.

S. XCII, vv. 18-21

...the orphan oppress not,
...the beggar drive not away,
...of the bounty of thy Lord be thy discourse.

S. XCIII, vv. 9-11

The alms are only for the poor and the needy, and those who collect them, and those whose hearts are to be reconciled,[1] and to free the captives and the debtors, and for the cause of Allah, and (for) the wayfarer; a duty imposed by Allah. Allah is Knower, Wise.

S. IX, v. 60

---

[1] A special portion of the alms was allotted to the people of Mecca, the former enemies of Al-Islam who were converted en masse after the capture of the city, and whose 'hearts were to be reconciled'.

10

TRUTH

Confound not truth with falsehood, nor knowingly conceal the truth.

S. II, v. 42

O ye who believe! Be careful of your duty to Allah, and be with the truthful.

S. IX, v. 119

And say: Truth hath come and falsehood hath vanished away. Lo! falsehood is ever bound to vanish.[1]

S. XVII, v. 81

...Shun lying speech...

S. XXII, v. 30

...And give good tidings (O Muhammad) to the good. Lo! Allah defendeth those who are true. Lo! Allah loveth not each treacherous ingrate.

S. XXII, vv. 37, 38

O ye who believe! Guard your duty to Allah, and speak words straight to the point.

S. XXXIII, v. 70

...Lo! Allah guideth not one who is a prodigal, a liar.

S. XL, v. 28

By the declining day,
Lo! man is in a state of loss,
Save those who believe and do good works, and exhort one another to truth and exhort one another to endurance.

S. CIII, vv. 1-3

---

1 These words were recited by the Prophet when he witnessed the destruction of idols round the Kabah after the conquest of Mecca.

11

FULFILMENT OF PLEDGES

...(The chosen of Allah is) he who fulfilleth his pledge and wardeth off (evil); for lo! Allah loveth those who ward off (evil).

S. III, v. 76

...break not your oaths after the asseveration of them, and after ve have made Allah surety over you. Lo! Allah knoweth what ye do.

S. XVI, v. 91

Successful indeed are the believers
...who are shepherds of their pledge and their covenant.

S. XXIII, v. 1, 8

...those who keep their pledges and their covenant,
And those who stand by their testimony
These will dwell in Gardens, honoured.

S. LXX, vv. 32, 33, 35

12

JUSTICE

And eat not up your property among yourselves in vanity, nor seek by it to gain the hearing of the judges that ye may knowingly devour a portion of the property of others wrongfully.

S. II, v. 188

O ye who believe! Be ye staunch in justice, witnesses for Allah, even though it be against yourselves or (your) parents or (your) kindred, whether (the case be of) a rich man or a poor man, for Allah is nearer unto both (than ye are). So follow not passion lest ye lapse (from truth) and if ye lapse or fall away, then lo! Allah is ever Informed of what ye do.

S. IV, v. 135

O ye who believe! Be steadfast witnesses for Allah in equity, and let not hatred of any people seduce you that ye deal not justly. Deal justly, that is nearer to your duty. Observe your duty to Allah. Lo! Allah is Informed of what ye do.

S. V, v. 8

And approach not the wealth of the orphan save with that which is better, till he reach maturity. Give full measure and full weight, in justice. We task not any soul beyond its scope. And if ye give your word, do justice thereunto, even though it be (against) a kinsman; and fulfil the covenant of Allah. This He commandeth you that haply ye may remember.

S. VI, v. 152

Say: My Lord enjoineth justice...

S. VII, v. 29

...Lo! Allah enjoineth justice and kindness...

S. XVI, v. 90

In that day (of Resurrection) their excuses will not profit those who did injustice, nor will they be allowed to make amends.

S. XXX, v. 57

...enjoin kindness and forbid iniquity...

S. XXXI, v. 17

...Lo! Allah loveth the just dealers.

S. LX, v. 8

And as for those who are unjust, they are firewood for hell.

S. LXXII, v. 15

And show not favour, seeking worldly gain!

S. LXXIV, v. 6

DEGREES OF RANK

He giveth wisdom unto whom He will, and he unto whom wisdom is given, he truly hath received abundant good. But none remember except men of understanding.

S. II, v. 269

And covet not the thing in which Allah hath made some of you excel others. Unto men a fortune from that which they have earned, and unto women a fortune from that which they have earned. (Envy not one another) but ask Allah of His bounty. Lo! Allah is ever Knower of all things.

S. IV, v. 32

...Allah hath conferred on those who strive with their wealth and lives a rank above the sedentary. Unto each Allah hath promised good, but He hath bestowed on those who strive a great reward above the sedentary;

Degrees of rank from Him, and forgiveness and mercy. Allah is ever Forgiving, Merciful.

S. IV, vv. 95, 96

He it is Who hath placed you as viceroys of the earth, and hath exalted some of you in rank above others, that He may try you by (the test of) that which He hath given you. Lo! Thy Lord is swift in prosecution, and Lo! He verily is Forgiving, Merciful.

S. VI, v. 165

ENVY

And covet not the thing in which Allah hath made some of you excel others. Unto men a fortune from that which they have earned, and unto women a fortune from that which they have earned. (Envy not one another) but ask Allah of His bounty. Lo! Allah is ever Knower of all things.

S. IV, v. 32

Say: I seek refuge in the Lord of Daybreak...
From the evil of the envier when he envieth.

S. CXIII, vv. 1, 5

Say: I seek refuge in the Lord of mankind,
The King of mankind,
The God of mankind,
From the evil of the sneaking whisperer,
Who whispereth in the hearts of mankind,
Of the jinn and of mankind.

S. CXIV, vv. 1-6

Here, says Pickthall, protection is sought especially from the evil in a man's own heart and in the hearts of other men.

PRIDE AND VANITY

Pride

...Lo! Allah loveth not such as are proud and boastful.

S. IV, v. 36

Your God is One God. But as for those who believe not in the Hereafter their hearts refuse to know, for they are proud.

Assuredly Allah knoweth that which they keep hidden and that which they proclaim. Lo! He loveth not the proud.

S. XVI, vv. 22, 23

...Woeful indeed will be the lodging of the arrogant.

S. XVI, v. 29

And walk not in the earth exultant. Lo! thou canst not rend the earth, nor canst thou stretch to the height of the hills.

S. XVII, v. 37

...Exult not; lo! Allah loveth not the exultant

S. XXVIII, v. 76

Turn not thy cheek in scorn toward folk, nor walk with pertness in the land. Lo! Allah loveth not each braggart boaster.

S. XXXI, v. 18

That ye grieve not for the sake of that which hath escaped you nor ye exult because of that which hath been given. Allah loveth not all prideful boasters.

S. LVII, v. 23

Vanity

O ye who believe! Squander not your wealth among yourselves in vanity...

S. IV, v. 29

Successful indeed are the believers
...who shun vain conversation

S. XXIII, vv. 1, 3

(The faithful slaves of the Beneficent are) those who will not witness vanity, but when they pass near senseless play, pass by with dignity.

S. XXV, v. 72

And when they hear of vanity they withdraw from it and say: Unto us our works and unto you your works. Peace be unto you! We desire not the ignorant.

S. XXVIII, v. 55

THE HUMBLE

Seek help in patience and prayer; and truly it is hard save for the humble-minded.

Who know that they will have to meet their Lord, and that unto Him they are returning.

S. II, vv. 45, 46

...give good tidings (O Muhammad) to the humble,

Whose hearts fear when Allah is mentioned, and the patient of whatever may befall them, and those who establish worship and who spend of that We have bestowed on them.

S. XXII, vv. 34, 35

...He is Best Aware of you (from the time) when He created you from the earth, and when ye were hidden in the bellies of your mothers. Therefor ascribe not purity unto yourselves. He is Best Aware of him who wardeth off (evil).

S. LIII, v. 32

Right Conduct

They believe in Allah and the Last Day, and enjoin right conduct and forbid indecency, and vie one with another in good works. These are of the righteous.

S. III, v. 114

...those who control their wrath and are forgiving toward mankind; Allah loveth the good;

S. III, v. 134

When ye are greeted with a greeting, greet ye with a better than it or return it. Lo! Allah taketh count of all things.

S. IV, v. 86

Allah loveth not the utterance of harsh speech save by one who hath been wronged. Allah is ever Hearer, Knower.

S. IV, v. 148

The (faithful) slaves of the Beneficent are they who walk upon the earth modestly, and when the foolish ones address them answer: Peace.

S. XXV, v. 63

Be modest in thy bearing and subdue thy voice. Lo! the harshest of all voices is the voice of the ass.

S. XXXI, v. 19

O ye who believe! Let not a folk deride a folk who may be better than they (are), nor let women (deride) women who may be better than they are; neither defame one another, nor insult one another by nicknames. Bad is the name of lewdness after faith. And whoso turneth not in repentance, such are evil-doers.

S. XLIX, v. 11

...Lo! the noblest of you, in the sight of Allah, is the best in conduct...

S. XLIX, v. 13

THE DISBELIEVERS

Lo! those who disbelieve and hinder (others) from the way of Allah, they verily have wandered far astray.

Lo! those who disbelieve and deal in wrong, Allah will never forgive them, neither will He guide them unto a road, Except the road of hell...

S. IV, vv. 167-169

And those who earn ill-déeds, (for them) requital of each ill-deed by the like thereof; and ignominy overtaketh them—They have no protector from Allah—as if their faces had been covered with a cloak of darkest night. Such are rightful owners of the Fire; they will abide therein.

S. X, v. 27

A similitude of those who disbelieve in their Lord: Their works are as ashes which the wind bloweth hard upon a stormy day. They have no control of aught that they have earned. That is the extreme failure.

S. XIV, v. 18

Whoso disbelieveth in Allah after his belief—save him who is forced thereto and whose heart is still content with the Faith—but whoso findeth ease in disbelief: On them is wrath from Allah. Theirs will be an awful doom.

That is because they have chosen the life of the world rather than the Hereafter, and because Allah guideth not the disbelieving folk.

Such are they whose hearts and ears and eyes Allah hath sealed. And such are the heedless.

S. XVI, vv. 106-108

Or have they chosen gods from the earth who raise the dead?

If there were therein gods beside Allah, then verily both (the heavens and the earth) had been disordered. Glorified be Allah, the Lord of the Throne, from all that they ascribe (unto Him).

S. XXI, vv. 21, 22

Say (unto them O Muhammad): I am only a mortal like you. It is inspired in me that your God is One God, therefor take the straight path unto Him and seek forgiveness of Him. And woe unto the idolators,

Who give not the poor-due, and who are disbelievers in the Hereafter.

S. XLI, vv. 6, 7

Or do those who commit ill-deeds suppose that We shall make them as those who believe and do good works, the same in life and death? Bad is their judgement!

Hast thou seen him who maketh his desire his god, and Allah sendeth him astray purposely, and sealeth up his hearing and his heart, and setteth on his sight a covering? Then who will lead him after Allah (hath condemned him)? Will ye not then heed?

S. XLV, vv. 21, 23

Lo! those who disbelieve and turn from the way of Allah and then die disbelievers, Allah surely will not pardon them.

S. XLVII, v. 34

Lo! thy Lord is Best Aware of him who strayeth from His way, and He is Best Aware of those who walk aright.

Therefor obey not thou the rejecters

Who would have had thee compromise, that they may compromise.

Neither obey thou each feeble oath-monger,

Detracter, spreader abroad of slanders,

Hinderer of the good, transgressor, malefactor

Greedy therewithal, intrusive.

S. LXVIII, vv. 7-13

Leave Me (to deal) with him whom I created lonely,

And then bestowed upon him ample means,

And sons abiding in his presence

And made (life) smooth for him.

Yet he desireth that I should give more.

Nay! For Lo! he hath been stubborn to Our revelations.

On him I shall impose a fearful doom.

For lo! he did consider; then he planned—

(Self-)destroyed is he, how he planned!

Again (self-)destroyed is he, how he planned!—

Then looked he,

Then frowned he and showed displeasure.

Then turned away in pride

And said: This is naught else than magic from of old; ·

This is naught else than speech of mortal man.

Him I shall fling unto the burning.

—Ah, what will convey unto thee what that burning is!—

It leaveth naught; it spareth naught

It shrivelleth the man.

S. LXXIV, vv. 11-29

Lo! these (disbelievers) love fleeting life, and put behind them (the remembrance of) a grievous day.

We, even We, created them, and strengthened their frame. And when We will, We can replace them, bringing others like them in their stead.

Lo! this is an Admonishment, that whosoever will may choose a way unto his Lord.

S. LXXVI, vv. 27-29

O man! what hath made thee careless concerning thy Lord, the Bountiful,

Who created thee, then fashioned, then proportioned thee?

Into whatsoever form He will, He casteth thee.

S. LXXXII, vv. 6-8

(By the) soul and Him who perfected it.

And inspired it (with conscience of) what is wrong for it and (what is) right for it.

He is indeed successful who causeth it to grow,

And he is indeed a failure who stunteth it.

S. XCI, vv. 7-10

Nay, but verily man is rebellious

That he thinketh himself independent!

Lo! unto thy Lord is the return.

Hast thou seen him who dissuadeth

A slave when he prayeth?

Hast thou seen if he (relieth) on the guidance (of Allah)

Or enjoineth piety?

Hast thou seen if he denieth (Allah's guidance) and is froward?

Is he then unaware that Allah seeth?

Nay, but if he cease not We will seize him by the fore-lock—

The lying, sinful forelock—

Then let him call upon his henchmen!

We will call the guards of hell.

Nay! Obey not thou him. But prostrate thyself, and draw near (unto Allah).

S. XCVI, vv. 6-19

Lo! those who disbelieve, among the People of the Scripture and the idolaters, will abide in fire of hell. They are the worst of created beings.

S. XCVIII, v. 6

PORTENTS

Lo! In the creation of the heavens and the earth and (in) the difference of night and day are tokens (of His Sovereignty) for men of understanding,

Such as remember Allah, standing, sitting, and reclining, and consider the creation of the heavens and the earth, (and say): Our Lord! Thou createdest not this in vain...

S. III, vv. 190,191

And if their aversion is grievous unto thee, then, if thou canst, seek a way down into the earth or a ladder unto the sky that thou mayst bring unto them a portent (to convince them all)!—If Allah willed, He could have brought them all together to the guidance—So be not thou among the foolish ones.

Only those can accept who hear...

They say: why hath no portent been sent down upon him from his Lord? Say: Lo! Allah is Able to send down a portent. But most of them know not.

S. VI, vv. 35-37

He it is Who sendeth down water from the sky, and therewith We bring forth buds of every kind; We bring forth the green blade from which We bring forth the thick-clustered grain; and from the date-palm, from the pollen thereof, spring pendant bunches; and (We bring forth) gardens of grapes, and the olive and the pomegranate, alike and unlike. Look upon the fruit thereof, when they bear fruit, and upon its ripening. Lo! herein verily are portents for a people who believe.

S. VI, v. 99

Proofs have come unto you from your Lord, so whoso seeth it is for his own good, and who is blind is blind to his own hurt. And I am not a keeper over you.

S. VI, v. 104

How many a portent is there in the heavens and the earth which they pass by with face averted!

S. XII, v. 105

Have not those who disbelieve known that the heavens and the earth were of one piece, then We parted them, and We made every living thing of water? Will they not then believe?

And We have placed in the earth firm hills lest it quake with them, and We have placed therein ravines as roads that haply they may find their way.

And We have made the sky a roof withheld (from them). Yet they turn away from its portents.

S. XXI, vv. 30-32

Man is made of haste. I shall show you My portents, but ask Me not to hasten.

S. XXI, v. 37

He bringeth forth the living from the dead, and He bringeth forth the dead from the living, and He reviveth the earth after her death. And even so will ye be brought forth.

And of His signs is this: He created you of dust, and behold you human beings, ranging widely!

And of His signs is this: He created for you helpmeets from yourselves that ye might find rest in them, and He ordained between you love and mercy. Lo, herein indeed are portents for folk who reflect.

And of His signs is the creation of the heavens and the earth, and the difference of your languages and colours. Lo! herein indeed are portents for men of knowledge.

S. XXX, vv. 19-22

And We created not the heaven and the earth and all that is between them in vain. That is the opinion of those who disbelieve. And woe unto those who disbelieve, from the Fire!

S. XXXVIII, v. 27

Assuredly the creation of the heavens and the earth is greater than the creation of mankind; but most of mankind know not.

S. XL, v. 57

And in the earth are portents for those whose faith is sure, And (also) in yourselves. Can ye then not see?

S. LI, vv. 20-21

HYPOCRISY AND TREACHERY

Hypocrisy

Bear unto the hypocrites the tidings that for them there is a painful doom;

S. IV, v. 138

Lo! the hypocrites (will be) in the lowest deep of the Fire, and thou wilt find no helper for them;

Save those who repent and amend and hold fast to Allah and make their religion pure for Allah (only). Those are with the believers. And Allah will bestow on the believers an immense reward.

S. IV, vv. 145,146

And incline not to the disbelievers and the hypocrites. Disregard their noxious talk, and put thy trust in Allah. Allah is sufficient as Trustee.

S. XXXIII, v. 48

Treachery

Lo! We reveal unto thee the Scripture with the truth, that thou mayst judge between mankind by that which Allah showeth thee. And be not thou a pleader for the treacherous;

And seek forgiveness of Allah. Lo! Allah is ever Forgiving, Merciful.

And plead not on behalf of (people) who deceive themselves. Lo! Allah loveth not one who is treacherous and sinful.

S. IV, vv. 105-107

Lo! the worst of beasts in Allah's sight are the ungrateful who will not believe;

Those of them with whom thou madest a treaty, and then at every opportunity they break their treaty, and they keep not duty (to Allah).

S. VIII, vv. 55, 56

Lo! Allah defendeth those who are true. Lo! Allah loveth not each treacherous ingrate.

S. XXII, v. 38

He knoweth the traitor of the eyes, and that which the bosoms hide.

S. XL, v. 19

LEWDNESS

They question thee about strong drink and games of chance. Say: In both is great sin and (some) utility for men; but the sin of them is greater than their usefulness.

S. II, v. 219

The devil promiseth you destitution and enjoineth on you lewdness. But Allah promiseth you forgiveness from Himself with bounty. Allah is All-Embracing, All-Knowing.

S. II, v. 268

Whoso committeth sin committeth it only against himself. Allah is ever Knower, Wise.

S. IV, v. 111

Forsake the outwardness of sin and the inwardness thereof. Lo! those who garner sin will be awarded that which they have earned.

S. VI, v. 120

Say: Come I will recite unto you that which your Lord hath made a sacred duty for you...that ye draw not nigh to lewd things whether open or concealed...

S. VI, v. 151

Say: My Lord forbiddeth only indecencies, such of them as are apparent and such as are within, and sin and wrongful oppression, and that ye associate with Allah that for which no warrant hath been revealed, and that ye tell concerning Allah that which ye know not.

S. VII, v. 33

Lo! Allah enjoineth justice and kindness, and giving to kinsfolk, and forbiddeth lewdness and abomination and wickedness. He exhorteth you in order that ye may take heed.

S. XVI, v. 90

And come not near unto adultery. Lo! it is an abomination and an evil way.

S. XVII, v. 32

HOARDING WEALTH

...That which they hoard will be their collar on the Day of Resurrection...

S. III, v. 180

...They who hoard up gold and silver and spend it not in the way of Allah, unto them give tidings (O Muhammad) of a painful doom.

S. IX, v. 34

Lo! ye are those who are called to spend in the way of Allah, yet among you there are some who hoard. And as for him who hoardeth, he hoardeth only from his soul. And Allah is the Rich, and ye are the poor. And if ye turn away He will exchange you for some other folk, and they will not be the likes of you.

S. XLVII, v. 38

It (fire of hell) calleth him who turned and fled (from truth),
And hoarded (wealth) and withheld it.

S. LXX, vv. 17, 18

As for him who giveth and is dutiful (toward Allah)
And believeth in goodness;
Surely We will ease his way unto the state of ease.
But as for him who hoardeth and deemeth himself independent,
And disbelieveth in goodness;
Surely We will ease his way unto adversity.
His riches will not save him when he perisheth.

S. XCII, vv. 5-11

THE PRODIGALS

...be not prodigal. Lo! Allah loveth not the prodigals.

S. VI, v. 141

O Children of Adam! Look to your adornment at every place of worship, and eat and drink, but be not prodigal. Lo! He loveth not the prodigals.

S. VII, v. 31

Say: O My slaves who have been prodigal to their own hurt! Despair not of the mercy of Allah, Who forgiveth all sins. Lo! He is the Forgiving, the Merciful.

S. XXXIX, v. 53

...Lo! Allah guideth not one who is a prodigal, a liar.

S. XL, v. 28

SLANDER

And whoso committeth a delinquency or crime, then throweth (the blame) thereof upon the innocent, hath burdened himself with falsehood and a flagrant crime.

S. IV, v. 112

And those who malign believing men and believing women undeservedly, they bear the guilt of slander and manifest sin.

S. XXXIII, v. 58

O ye who believe! Let not a folk deride a folk who may be better than they (are), nor let women (deride) women who may be better than they are; neither defame one another, nor insult one another by nicknames. Bad is the name of lewdness after faith. And whoso turneth not in repentance, such are evildoers.

O ye who believe! Shun much suspicion; for lo! some suspicion is a crime. And spy not, neither backbite one another...

S. XLIX, vv. 11, 12

Neither obey thou each feeble oath-monger,
Detractor, spreader abroad of slanders.

S. LXVIII, vv. 10, 11

Woe unto every slandering traducer,
Who hath gathered wealth (of this world) and arranged it.
He thinketh that his wealth will render him immortal.
Nay, but verily he will be flung to the Consuming One.
Ah, what will convey unto thee what the Consuming One is!
(It is) the fire of Allah, kindled,
Which leapeth up over the hearts (of men).
Lo! it is closed in on them
In outstretched columns.

S. CIV, vv. 1-9

24

THE DEFRAUDERS

Give unto orphans their wealth. Exchange not the good for the bad (in your management thereof) nor absorb their wealth into your own wealth. Lo! that would be a great sin.

S. IV, v. 2

Lo! Those who devour the wealth of orphans wrongfully, they do but swallow fire into their bellies, and they will be exposed to burning flame.

S. IV, v. 10

Come not near the wealth of the orphan save with that which is better till he come to strength; and keep the covenant. Lo! of the covenant it will be asked.

S. XVII, v. 34

...Lo! a clear proof hath come unto you from your Lord; so give full measure and full weight and wrong.not mankind in their goods, and work not confusion in the earth after the fair ordering thereof. That will be better for you, if ye are believers.

S. VII, v. 85

O my people! Give full measure and full weight in justice, and wrong not people in respect of their goods. And do not evil in the earth, causing corruption.

S. XI, v. 85

Fill the measure when ye measure, and weigh with a right balance; that is meet, and better in the end.

S. XVII, v. 35

Give full measure and be not of those who give less (than the due).

And weigh with the true balance.

Wrong not mankind in their goods, and do not evil, making mischief, in the earth.

S. XXVI, vv. 181-183

Woe unto the defrauders:

Those who when they take the measure from mankind demand it full,

But if they measure unto them or weigh for them, they cause them loss.

Do such (men) not consider that they will be raised again

Unto an Awful Day,

The day when (all) mankind stand before the Lord of the Worlds?

S. LXXXIII, vv. 1-6

MAN'S INFIRMITY

Allah tasketh not a soul beyond its scope...

S. II, v. 286

Allah would make the burden light for you, for man was created weak.

S. IV, v. 28

And if misfortune touch a man he crieth unto Us, (while reclining) on his side, or sitting or standing, but when We have relieved him of the misfortune he goeth his way as though he had not cried unto Us because of a misfortune that afflicted him. Thus is what they do made (seeming) fair unto the prodigal.

S. X, v. 12

And He giveth you of all ye ask of Him, and if ye would count the bounty of Allah ye cannot reckon it. Lo! man is verily a wrong-doer, an ingrate.

S. XIV, v. 34

And if We cause man to taste some mercy from Us and afterward withdraw it from him, lo! he is despairing, thankless.

And if We cause him to taste grace after some misfortune that had befallen him, he saith: The ills have gone from me. Lo! he is exultant, boastful;

Save those who persevere and do good works. Theirs will be forgiveness and a great reward.

S. XI, vv. 9-11

Man prayeth for evil as he prayeth for good; for man was ever hasty.

S. XVII, v. 11

And when We make life pleasant unto man, he turneth away and is averse; and when ill toucheth him he is in despair.

S. XVII, v. 83

And when some hurt toucheth man, he crieth unto his Lord, turning unto Him (repentant). Then, when He granteth him a boon from Him he forgetteth that for which he cried

unto Him before, and setteth up rivals to Allah that he may
beguile (men) from His way. Say (O Muhammad, unto such
an one): Take pleasure in thy disbelief a while. Lo! thou art
of the owners of the Fire.

S. XXXIX, v. 8

Man tireth not of praying for good, and if ill toucheth
him, then he is disheartened, desperate.

S. XLI, v. 49

When We show favour unto man, he withdraweth and
turneth aside, but when ill toucheth him then he aboundeth
in prayer.

S. XLI, v. 51

...And lo! when We cause man to taste of mercy from Us
he exulteth therefor. And if some evil striketh them because
of that which their own hands have sent before, then lo!
man is an ingrate.

S. XLII, v. 48

Lo! man was created anxious,
Fretful when evil befalleth him
And, when good befalleth him, grudging;
Save worshippers
Who are constant at their worship

S. LXX, vv. 19-23

As for man, whenever his Lord trieth him by honouring
him, and is gracious unto him, he saith: My Lord honoureth
me.

But whenever He trieth him by straitening his means
of life, he saith: My Lord despiseth me.

Nay, but ye (for your part) honour not the orphan
And urge not on the feeding of the poor,
And ye devour heritages with devouring greed,
And love wealth with abounding love.

S. LXXXIX, vv. 15-20

Lo! man is an ingrate unto his Lord.

S. C, v. 6

REPENTANCE

And those who, when they do an evil thing or wrong themselves, remember Allah and implore forgiveness for their sins — Who forgiveth sins save Allah only?—and will not knowingly repeat (the wrong) they did.

The reward of such will be forgiveness from their Lord, and Gardens underneath which rivers flow, wherein they will abide for ever—a bountiful reward for workers!

S. III, vv. 135, 136

Yet whoso doeth evil or wrongeth his own soul, then seeketh pardon of Allah, will find Allah Forgiving, Merciful.

S. IV, v. 110

And when those who believe in Our revelations come unto thee, say: Peace be unto you! Your Lord hath prescribed for Himself mercy, that whoso of you doeth evil (through ignorance) and repenteth afterward thereof and doeth right, (for him) lo! He is Forgiving, Merciful.

S. VI, v. 54

But those who do ill-deeds and afterward repent and believe—lo! for them afterward, Allah is Forgiving, Merciful.

S. VII, v. 153

Ask pardon of your Lord and then turn unto Him (repentant). Lo! my Lord is Merciful, Loving.

S. XI, v. 90

Then lo! thy Lord—for those who do evil in ignorance and afterward repent and amend—lo! (for them) thy Lord is afterward indeed Forgiving, Merciful.

S. XVI, v. 119

And lo! verily I am Forgiving toward him who repenteth and believeth and doeth good, and afterward walketh aright.

S. XX, v. 82

Turn unto your Lord repentant, and surrender unto Him, before there come unto you the doom, when ye cannot be helped.

S. XXXIX, v. 54

And He it is who accepteth repentance from His bondmen, and pardoneth the evil deeds, and knoweth what ye do,

And accepteth those who do good works, and giveth increase unto them of His bounty. And as for disbelievers, theirs will be an awful doom.

S. XLII, vv. 25, 26

FORGIVENESS AND MERCY

Forgiveness

A kind word with forgiveness is better than alms-giving followed by injury...

S. II, v. 263

Keep to forgiveness (O Muhammad), and enjoin kindness and turn away from the ignorant.

S. VII, v. 199

O ye who believe! If ye keep your duty to Allah, He will give you discrimination (between right and wrong) and will rid you of your evil thoughts and deeds, and will forgive you. Allah is of Infinite Bounty.

S. VIII, v. 29

If Allah were to hasten on for men the ill (that they have earned) as they would hasten on the good, their respite would already have expired. But We suffer those who look not for the meeting with Us to wander blindly on in their contumacy.

S. X, v. 11

And if ye would count the favour of Allah ye cannot reckon it. Lo! Allah is indeed Forgiving, Merciful.

S. XVI, v. 18

If Allah were to take mankind to task for their wrong-doing, He would not leave hereon a living creature, but He reprieveth them to an appointed term, and when their term cometh they cannot put (it) off an hour nor (yet) advance (it).

S. XVI, v. 61

Whosoever goeth right, it is only for (the good of) his own soul that he goeth right, and whosoever erreth, erreth only to its hurt. No laden soul can bear another's load. We never punish until We have sent a messenger.

S. XVII, v. 15

Whatever of misfortune striketh you, it is what your right hands have earned. And He forgiveth much.

S. XLII, v. 30

And those who shun the worst of sins and indecencies and, when they are wroth, forgive,

And those who answer the call of their Lord and establish worship and whose affairs are a matter of counsel, and who spend of what We have bestowed on them,

And those who, when great wrong is done to them, defend themselves,

The guerdon of an ill-deed is an ill the like thereof. But whosoever pardoneth and amendeth, his wage is the affair of Allah. Lo! Allah loveth not wrong-doers.

S. XLII,.vv. 37-40

Mercy

...Allah would turn to you in mercy; but those who follow vain desires would have you go tremendously astray.

Allah will make the burden light for you, for man was created weak.

S. IV, vv. 27, 28

If ye avoid the great (things) which ye are forbidden, We will remit from you your evil deeds and make you enter at a noble gate.

S. IV, v. 31

Yet whoso doeth evil or wrongeth his own soul, then seeketh pardon of Allah, will find Allah Forgiving, Merciful.

S. IV, v. 110

And when those who believe in Our revelations come unto thee, say: Peace be unto you! Your Lord hath prescribed for Himself mercy, that whoso of you doeth evil through ignorance and repenteth afterward thereof and doeth right, (for him) lo! He is Forgiving, Merciful.

S. VI, v. 54

Work not confusion in the earth after the fair ordering (thereof), and call on Him in fear and hope. Lo! the mercy of Allah is nigh unto the good.

S. VII, v. 56

...there is no sin for you in the mistakes that ye make unintentionally, but what your hearts purpose (that will be a sin for you). Allah is ever Forgiving, Merciful.

S. XXXIII, v. 5

Whoso doeth right it is for his soul, and whoso doeth wrong it is against it. And thy Lord is not at all a tyrant to His slaves.

S. XLI, v. 46

Those who avoid enormities of sin and abominations, save the unwilled offences—(for them) lo! thy Lord is of vast mercy...

S. LIII, v. 32

JESUS

Pickthall notes in the introduction to Surah XIX:

In the fifth year of the Prophet's mission a number of the poorer converts were allowed by the Prophet to emigrate to Abyssinia, a Christian country where they would not be subject to persecution for their worship of the One God. The rulers of Mecca sent ambassadors to ask the Negus for their extradition, accusing them of having left the religion of their own people without entering the Christian religion, and of having done wrong in their own country. The Negus (against the wish of the envoys) sent for the spokesmen of the refugees and, in the presence of the bishops of his realm, questioned them of their religion. Jafar ibn Abi Talib, cousin of the Prophet, answered:

'We were folk immersed in ignorance, worshipping idols, eating carrion, given to lewdness, severing the ties of kinship, bad neighbours, the strong among us preying the weak; thus were we till Allah sent to us a messenger of our own, whose lineage, honesty, trustworthiness and chastity we knew, and he called us to Allah that we should acknowledge His unity and worship Him and eschew all the stones and idols that we and our fathers used to worship beside Him; and ordered us to be truthful and to restore the pledge and observe the ties of kinship, and be good neighbours, and to abstain from things forbidden, and from blood, and forbade us lewdness and false speech, and to prey upon the wealth of orphans, and to accuse good women; and commanded us to worship Allah only, ascribing no thing unto Him as partner, and enjoined upon us prayer and legal alms and fasting. (And he enumerated for him the teachings of Islam).

'So we trusted him and we believed in him and followed that which he had brought from Allah, and we worshipped Allah only, and ascribed no thing as partner unto Him. And we refrained from that which was forbidden to us, and indulged in that which was made lawful for us. And our people became hostile to us and tormented us, and sought to turn us from our religion that they might bring us back to the worship of idols from the worship of Allah Most High, and that we might indulge in those iniquities which before we had deemed lawful.

'And when they persecuted and oppressed us, and hemmed us in, and kept us from the practice of our religion, we came forth to thy land, and chose thee above all others, and sought thy protection, and hoped that we should not be troubled in thy land, O King!'

Then the Negus asked him: Hast with thee aught of that which he brought from Allah? Jafar answered: Yes. Then the Negus said: Relate it to me, and Jafar recited to him the beginning of Surah XIX, entitled, MARY.

This Surah also deals with the birth of Jesus.

And when the angels said: O Mary! Lo! Allah hath chosen thee and made thee pure, and hath preferred thee above (all) the women of creation.

O Mary! Be obedient to thy Lord, prostrate thyself and bow with those who bow (in worship).

This is of the tidings of things hidden. We reveal it unto thee (Muhammad). Thou wast not present with them when they threw their pens (to know) which of them should be the guardian of Mary, nor wast thou present with them when they quarrelled (thereupon).

(And remember) when the angels said: O Mary! Lo! Allah giveth thee glad tidings of a word from Him, whose name is the Messiah, Jesus, son of Mary, illustrious in the world and the Hereafter, and one of those brought near (unto Allah).

He will speak unto mankind in his cradle and in his manhood, and he is of the righteous.

She said: My Lord! How can I have a child when no mortal hath touched me? He said: So (it will be). Allah createth what He will. If He decreeth a thing, He saith unto it only: Be! and it is.

And He will teach him the Scripture and wisdom, and the Torah and the Gospel.

S. III, vv. 42-48

Then she brought him to her own folk, carrying him.
They said: O Mary! thou hast come with an amazing thing.

Oh sister of Aaron! thy father was not a wicked man nor
was thy mother a harlot.

Then she pointed to him. They said: How can we talk to
one who is in the cradle, a young boy?

He spake: Lo! I am the slave of Allah. He hath given me
the Scripture and hath appointed me a Prophet.

And hath made me blessed wheresoever I may be, and
hath enjoined upon me prayer and almsgiving so long as I
remain alive,

And (hath made me) dutiful toward her who bore me,
and hath not made me arrogant, unblest.

Peace on me the day I was born, and the day I die, and
the day I shall be raised alive!

Such was Jesus, son of Mary: (this is) a statement of the
truth concerning which they doubt.

S. XIX, vv. 27-34

And verily We gave unto Moses the Scripture and We
caused a train of messengers to follow after him, and We
gave unto Jesus, son of Mary, clear proofs (of Allah's sovereignty), and We supported him with the holy Spirit.[1]
Is it ever so, that, when there cometh unto you a messenger
(from Allah) with that which ye yourselves desire not, ye
grow arrogant, and some ye disbelieve and some ye slay?

S. II, v. 87

(And remember) when Allah said: O Jesus! Lo! I am
gathering thee and causing thee to ascend unto Me, and am
cleansing thee of those who disbelieve and am setting those
who follow thee above those who disbelieve until the Day
of Resurrection. Then unto Me ye will (all) return, and I
shall judge between you as to that wherein ye used to differ.

S. III, v. 55

And because of their[2] disbelief and of their speaking
against Mary a tremendous calumny;

And because of their saying: We slew the Messiah, Jesus
son of Mary, Allah's messenger—They slew him not nor

[1] 'The holy Spirit' is a term for the angel of Revelation, Gabriel (on whom be
peace).

[2] Reference is to the Jews.

crucified him, but it appeared so unto them; and lo! those who disagree concerning it are in doubt thereof; they have no knowledge thereof save pursuit of a conjecture; they slew him not for certain,

But Allah took him up unto Himself. Allah was ever Mighty, Wise.

S. IV, vv. 156-158

O People of the Scripture! Do not exaggerate in your religion nor utter aught concerning Allah save the truth. The Messiah, Jesus son of Mary, was only a messenger of Allah, and His word which He conveyed unto Mary, and a spirit from Him. So believe in Allah and His messengers, and say not 'Three'—Cease! (it is) better for you!—Allah is only one God. Far is it removed from His Transcendant Majesty that He should have a son. His is all that is in the heavens and all that is in the earth. And Allah is sufficient as Defender.

S. IV, v. 171

And We caused Jesus, son of Mary, to follow in their[1] footsteps, confirming that which was (revealed) before him, and We bestowed on him the Gospel wherein is guidance and a light, confirming that which was (revealed) before it in the Torah—a guidance and an admonition unto those who ward off (evil)

Let the People of the Gospel judge by that which Allah hath revealed therein. Whoso judgeth not by that which Allah hath revealed; such are evil-livers.

S. V, vv. 46, 47

When Allah saith: O Jesus, son of Mary! Remember My favour unto thee and unto thy mother; how I strengthened thee with the holy Spirit, so that thou spakest unto mankind in the cradle as in maturity; and how I taught thee the Scripture and Wisdom and the Torah and the Gospel; and how thou didst shape of clay as it were the likeness of a bird by My permission, and didst blow upon it and it was a bird by My permission and thou didst heal him who was born blind and the leper by My permission; and how thou didst raise the dead, by My permission; and how I restrained the children of Israel from (harming) thee when thou camest

---

[1] Reference is to Prophets to whom the Torah was revealed.

unto them with clear proofs, and those of them who disbelieved exclaimed: This is naught else than mere magic;

And when I inspired the disciples, (saying): Believe in Me
and in My messenger, they said: We believe. Bear witness
that we have surrendered[1] (unto Thee).

S. V, vv. 110, 111

And when Allah saith: O Jesus, son of Mary! Didst thou
say unto mankind: Take me and my mother for two gods
beside Allah? he saith: Be glorified! It was not mine to utter
that to which I had no right. If I used to say it, then Thou
knewest it. Thou knowest what is in my mind, and I know
not what is in Thy mind. Lo! Thou, only Thou art the
Knower of Things Hidden.

I spake unto them only that which Thou commandedst
me, (saying): Worship Allah, my Lord and your Lord. I was
a witness of them while I dwelt among them, and when
Thou tookest me Thou wast the Watcher over them. Thou
art Witness over all things.

If Thou punish them, lo! they are Thy slaves, and if
Thou forgive them (lo! they are Thy slaves). Lo! Thou,
only Thou art the Mighty, the Wise.

Allah saith: This is a day in which their truthfulness
profiteth the truthful, for theirs are Gardens underneath
which rivers flow, wherein they are secure for ever, Allah
taking pleasure in them and they in Him. That is the great
triumph.

Unto Allah belongeth the Sovereignty of the heavens
and the earth and whatsoever is therein, and He is Able to
do all things.

S. V, vv. 116-120

It befitteth not (the Majesty of) Allah that He should
take unto Himself a son, Glory be to Him! When He decreeth
a thing, He saith unto it only: Be! and it is.

And Lo! Allah is my Lord and your Lord. So serve Him.
That is the right path.

S. XIX, vv. 35, 36

And they say: The Beneficent hath taken unto Himself
a son.

---

1 or 'are Muslims'

Assuredly ye utter a disastrous thing,

Whereby almost the heavens are torn, and the earth is split asunder and the mountains fall in ruins,

That ye ascribe unto the Beneficent a son,

When it is not meet for (the Majesty of) the Beneficent that He should choose a son.

There is none in the heavens and the earth but cometh unto the Beneficent as a slave.

S. XIX, vv. 88-93

Say (O Muhammad): The Beneficent One hath no son...

S. XLIII, v. 81

NO DISTINCTION BETWEEEN ALLAH'S MESSENGERS

Say (O Muslims): We believe in Allah and that which is revealed unto us and that which was revealed unto Abraham, and Ishmael, and Isaac, and Jacob, and the tribes, and that which Moses and Jesus received, and that which the prophets received from their Lord. We make no distinction between any of them, and unto Him we have surrendered.

S. II, v. 136

The messenger believeth in that which hath been revealed unto him from his Lord and (so do) the believers. Each one believeth in Allah and His angels and His scriptures and His messengers—We make no distinction between any of His messengers—and they say: We hear, and we obey. (Grant us) Thy forgiveness, our Lord. Unto Thee is the journeying.

S. II, v. 285

Lo! those who disbelieve in Allah and His messengers, and seek to make distinction between Allah and His messengers, and say: We believe in some and disbelieve in others, and seek to choose a way in between;

Such are disbelievers in truth; and for disbelievers We prepare a shameful doom.

But those who believe in Allah and His messengers and make no distinction between any of them, unto them Allah will give their wages; and Allah was ever Forgiving, Merciful.

S. IV, vv. 150-152

But those of them who are firm in knowledge and the believers believe in that which is revealed unto thee, and that which was revealed before thee, especially the diligent in prayer and those who pay the poor-due, the believers in Allah and the Last Day. Upon these We shall bestow immense reward.

S. IV, v. 162

PEOPLE OF THE SCRIPTURE

Enjoin ye righteousness upon mankind while ye yourselves forget (to practise it)? And ye are readers of the Scripture! Have ye then no sense?

S. II, v. 44

Lo! those who believe (in that which is revealed unto thee Muhammad), and those who are Jews, and Christians, and Sabaeans—whoever believeth in Allah and the Last Day and doeth right—surely their reward is with their Lord, and there shall no fear come upon them neither shall they grieve.

S. II, v. 62

Those unto whom We have given the Scripture, who read it with the right reading, those believe in it. And whoso disbelieveth in it, those are they who are the losers.

S. II, v. 121

And they say: Be Jews or Christians, then ye will be rightly guided. Say (unto them, O Muhammad): Nay, but (we follow) the religion of Abraham, the upright, and he was not of the idolaters.

S. II, v. 135

And if they believe in the like of that which ye believe, then are they rightly guided. But if they turn away, then are they in schism, and Allah will suffice thee (for defence) against them. He is the Hearer, the Knower.

(We take our) colour from Allah, and who is better than Allah at colouring. We are His worshippers.

Say (unto the People of the Scripture): Dispute ye with us concerning Allah when He is our Lord and your Lord? Ours are our works and yours your works. We look to Him alone.

S. II, vv. 137-139

Mankind were one community, and Allah sent (unto them) prophets as bearers of good tidings and as warners, and revealed therewith the Scripture with the truth that it might judge between mankind concerning that wherein they differed. And only those unto whom (the Scripture) was given differed concerning it, after clear proofs had come unto them, through hatred one of another. And Allah by His Will guided those who believe unto the truth of that concerning which they differed. Allah guideth whom He will unto a straight path.

S. II, v. 213

And Lo! of the People of the Scripture there are some who believe in Allah and that which is revealed unto you and that which was revealed unto them, humbling themselves before Allah. They purchase not a trifling gain at the price of the revelations of Allah. Verily their reward is with their Lord. Lo! Allah is swift to take account.

S. III, v. 199

And with those who say: 'Lo! we are Christians', We made a covenant, but they forgot a part of that whereof they were admonished. Therefor We have stirred up enmity and hatred among them till the Day of Resurrection, when Allah will inform them of their handiwork.

O people of the Scripture! Now hath Our messenger come unto you, expounding unto you much of that which ye used to hide in the Scriputre, and forgiving much. Now hath come unto you light from Allah and a plain Scripture,

Whereby Allah guideth him who seeketh His good pleasure unto paths of peace. He bringeth them out of darkness unto light by His decree, and guideth them unto a straight path.

S. V, vv. 14-16

Lo! We did reveal the Torah, wherein is guidance and a light, by which the prophets who surrendered (unto Allah) judged the Jews, and the rabbis and the priests (judged) by such of Allah's Scripture as they were bidden to observe, and thereunto were they witnesses. So fear not mankind, but fear Me. And barter not My revelations for a little gain. Whoso judgeth not by that which Allah hath revealed: such are disbelievers.

S. V, v. 44

And unto thee have We revealed the Scripture with the truth, confirming whatever Scripture was before it, and a watcher over it. So judge between them by that which Allah hath revealed, and follow not their desires away from the

Truth which hath come unto thee. For each We have appointed a divine law and a traced-out way. Had Allah willed He
could have made you one community. But that He may try
you by that which He hath given you (He hath made you as
ye are). So vie one with another in good works. Unto Allah
ye will all return, and He will then inform you of that wherein ye differ.

S. V, v. 48

If only the People of the Scripture would believe and
ward off (evil), surely We should remit their sins from them
and surely We should bring them into Gardens of Delight.

S. V, v. 65

Say: O People of the Scripture! Ye have naught (of guidance) till ye observe the Torah and the Gospel and that
which was revealed unto you from your Lord. That which
is revealed unto thee (Muhammad) from thy Lord is certain
to increase the contumacy and disbelief of many of them.
But grieve not for the disbelieving folk.

Lo! those who believe, and those who are Jews, and
Sabaeans and Christians—Whosoever believeth in Allah and
the Last Day and doeth right—there shall no fear come upon
them neither shall they grieve.

S. V, vv. 68, 69

Thou wilt find the most vehement of mankind in hostility
to those who believe (to be) the Jews and the idolaters. And
thou wilt find the nearest of them in affection to those
who believe (to be) those who say: Lo! We are Christians.
That is because there are among them priests and monks,[1]
and because they are not proud.

S.V, v. 82

And argue not with the People of the Scripture unless it
be in (a way) that is better, save with such of them as do
wrong; and say: We believe in that which hath been revealed
unto us and revealed unto you; our God and your God is
One, and Unto him we surrender.

S. XXIX, v. 46

Lo! those who read the Scripture of Allah, and establish
worship, and spend of that which we have bestowed on them
secretly and openly, they look forward to imperishable gain,

---

[1] i.e. persons entirely devoted to the service of God, as were the Muslims.

That He will pay them their wages and increase them of His grace. Lo! He is Forgiving, Responsive.

As for that which We inspire in thee of the Scripture, it is the Truth confirming that which was (revealed) before it. Lo! Allah is indeed Observer, Seer of His slaves.

S. XXXV, vv. 29-31

And We verily gave Moses the guidance, and we caused the children of Israel to inherit the Scripture,

A guide and a reminder for men of understanding.

Then have patience (O Muhammad). Lo! the promise of Allah is true. And ask forgiveness of thy sin, and hymn the praise of thy Lord at fall of night and in the early hours.

Lo! those who wrangle concerning the revelations of Allah without a warrant having come unto them, there is naught else in their breasts save pride which they will never attain. So take thou refuge in Allah. Lo! He, only He, is the Hearer, the Seer.

S. XL, vv. 53-56

...say: I believe in whatever Scripture Allah hath sent down, and I am commanded to be just among you. Allah is our Lord and your Lord. Unto us our works and unto you your works; no argument between us and you. Allah will bring us together, and unto Him is the journeying.

S. XLII, v. 15

THE SCHISMATICS

And hold fast, all of you together, to the cable of Allah, and do not separate...

S. III, v. 103

Lo! As for those who sunder their religion and become schismatics, no concern at all hast thou with them. Their case will go to Allah, Who then will tell them what they used to do.

S. VI, v. 159

...dispute not with one another lest ye falter and your strength depart from you; but be steadfast! Lo! Allah is with the steadfast.

S. VIII, v. 46

Lo! this, your religion, is one religion, and I am your Lord, so worship Me.

And they have broken their religion (into fragments) among them, (yet) all are returning unto Us.

Then whoso doeth good works and is a believer, there will be no rejection of his effort. Lo! We record (it) for him.

S. XXI, vv. 92-94

(Be not) of those who split up religion and became schismatics, each sect exulting in its tenets.

S. XXX, v. 32

The believers are naught else than brothers. Therefore make peace between your brethren and observe your duty to Allah that haply ye may obtain mercy.

S. XLIX, v. 10

NO COMPULSION IN RELIGION

There is no compulsion in religion...

S. II, v. 256

And if they believe in the like of that which ye believe, then are they rightly guided. But if they turn away, then are they in schism, and Allah will suffice thee (for defence) against them. He is the Hearer, the Knower.

(We take our) colour from Allah, and who is better than Allah at colouring. We are His worshippers.

Say (unto the People of the Scripture): Dispute ye with us concerning Allah when He is our Lord and your Lord? Ours are our works and yours your works. We look to Him alone.

S. II, vv. 137-139

Obey Allah and obey the messenger, and beware! But if ye turn away, then know that the duty of Our messenger is only plain conveyance (of the message).

S. V, v. 92

Proofs have come unto you from your Lord, so whoso seeth, it is for his own good, and whoso is blind is blind to his own hurt. And I am not a keeper over you.

S. VI, v. 104

Revile not those unto whom they pray beside Allah lest they wrongfully revile Allah through ignorance. Thus unto every nation have We made their deed seem fair. Then unto their Lord is their return, and He will tell them what they used to do.

S. VI, v. 108

And if they deny thee, say: unto me my work, and unto you your work. Ye are innocent of what I do, and I am innocent of what ye do.

S. X, v. 41

And if thy Lord willed, all who are in the earth would have believed together. Wouldst thou (Muhammad) compel men until they are believers?

S. X, v. 99

Call unto the way of thy Lord with wisdom and fair exhortation, and reason with them, in the better way. Lo! thy Lord is Best Aware of him who strayeth from His way, and He is Best Aware of those who go aright.

S. XVI, v. 125

Say: (The Quran is) the truth from the Lord of you (all). Then whosoever will, let him believe, and whosoever will, let him disbelieve...

S. XVIII, v. 29

And we have sent thee (O Muhammad) only as a bearer of good tidings and a warner.

S. XXV, v. 56

...And be thou upright as thou art commanded, and follow not their lusts, but say: I believe in whatever scripture Allah hath sent down, and I am commanded to be just among you. Allah is our Lord and your Lord. Unto us our works and unto you your works; no argument between us and you. Allah will bring us together and unto Him is the journeying.

S. XLII, v. 15

Tolerance

And he saith: O my Lord: Lo! those are a folk who believe not.

Then bear with them (O Muhammad) and say: Peace. But they will come to know.

S. XLIII, vv. 88, 89

Lord of the East and the West; there is no God save Him; so choose thou Him alone for thy defender.

And bear with patience what they utter, and part from them with a fair leave-taking.

S. LXXIII, vv. 9, 10

Say: O disbelievers!
I worship not that which ye worship;
Nor worship ye that which I worship.
And I shall not worship that which ye worship.
Nor will ye worship that which I worship.
Unto you your religion, and unto me my religion.

S. CIX, vv. 1-6

PEACE

And make not Allah, by your oaths, a hindrance to your being righteous and observing your duty unto Him and making peace among mankind...

S. II, v. 224

Whoso interveneth in a good cause will have the reward thereof, and whoso interveneth in an evil cause will bear the consequence thereof. Allah overseeth all things.

S. IV, v. 85

There is no good in much of their secret conferences save (in) him who enjoineth almsgiving and kindness and peace-making among the people. Whoso doeth that, seeking the good pleasure of Allah, We shall bestow on him a vast reward.

S. IV, v. 114

Work not confusion in the earth after the fair ordering (thereof), and call on Him in fear and hope. Lo! the mercy of Allah is nigh unto the good.

S. VII, v. 56

...and work not confusion in the earth after the fair ordering thereof. That will be better for you, if ye are believers.

S. VII, v. 85

Aggression

Fight in the way of Allah against those who fight against you, but begin not hostilities. Lo! Allah loveth not aggressors.

S. II, v. 190

...kill not one another. Lo! Allah is ever Merciful unto you.

Whoso doeth that through aggression and injustice, We shall cast him into Fire, and that is ever easy for Allah.

S. IV, vv. 29, 30

(O mankind!) Call upon your Lord humbly and in secret. Lo! He loveth not aggressors.

S. VII, v. 55

CORRUPTION

...And do not evil in the earth, causing corruption.

S. XI, v. 85

...obey not the command of the prodigal,
Who spread corruption in the earth, and reform not.

.S. XXVI, vv. 151, 152

...and do not evil, making mischief, in the earth.

S. XXVI, v. 183

But seek the abode of the Hereafter in that which Allah hath given thee and neglect not thy portion of the world, and be thou kind even as Allah hath been kind to thee, and seek not corruption in the earth; lo! Allah loveth not corrupters.

S. XXVIII, v. 77

Shall We treat those who believe and do good works as those who spread corruption in the earth; or shall We treat the pious as the wicked?

S. XXXVIII, v. 28

Oppression

Say: My Lord forbiddeth only indecencies, such of them as are apparent and such as are within, and sin and wrongful oppression, and that ye associate with Allah that for which no warrant hath been revealed, and that ye tell concerning Allah that which ye know not.

S. VII, v. 33

The way (of blame) is only against those who oppress mankind, and wrongfully rebel in the earth. For such there is a painful doom.

And verily whoso is patient and forgiveth—lo! that, verily, is (of) the steadfast heart of things.

S. XLII, vv. 42, 43

RISE AND FALL OF NATIONS

Systems have passed away before you. Do but travel in the land and see the nature of the consequence for those who did deny (the messengers).

This is a declaration for mankind, a guidance and an admonition unto those who ward off (evil).

S. III, vv. 137, 138

See they not how many a generation We destroyed before them, whom We had established in the earth more firmly than We have established you, and We shed on them abundant showers from the sky, and made the rivers flow beneath them. Yet we destroyed them for their sins, and created after them another generation.

S. VI, v. 6

And every nation hath its term, and when its term cometh, they cannot put if off an hour nor yet advance (it).

S. VII, v. 34

...Lo! Allah changeth not the condition of a folk until they (first) change that which is in their hearts...

S. XIII, v. 11

Is it not guidance for them (to know) how many a generation We destroyed before them, amid whose dwellings they walk? Lo! therein verily are signs for men of thought.

S. XX, v. 128

No nation can outstrip its term, nor yet postpone it.

S. XXIII, v. 43

If Allah took mankind to task by that which they deserve, He would not leave a living creature on the surface of the earth; but He reprieveth them unto an appointed term, and when their term cometh—then verily (they will know that) Allah is ever Seer of His slaves.

S. XXXV, v. 45

Have they not travelled in the land to see the nature of the consequence for those before them? They were more numerous than these, and mightier in power and (in the) traces (which they left behind them) in the earth. But all that they used to earn availed them not.

S. XL, v. 82

EVOLUTION

There is not an animal in the earth, nor a flying creature flying on two wings, but they are peoples like unto you...

S. VI, v. 38

See they not how Allah produceth creation, then reproduceth it? Lo! for Allah that is easy.

Say (O Muhammad): Travel in the land and see how He originated creation, then Allah bringeth forth the later growth. Lo! Allah is Able to do all things.

S. XXIX, vv. 19, 20

Glory be to Him Who created all the sexual pairs, of that which the earth groweth, and of themselves, and of that which they know not!

S. XXXVI, v. 36

What aileth you that ye hope not toward Allah for dignity When He created you by (divers) stages?

S. LXXI, vv. 13, 14

Oh, I swear by the afterglow of sunset,
And by the night and all that it enshroudeth,
And by the moon when she is at the full,
That ye shall journey on from plane to plane.

S. LXXXIV, vv. 16-19

LIFE OF THIS WORLD

Beautified is the life of the world for those who disbelieve; they make a jest of the believers. But those who keep their duty to Allah will be above them on the Day of Resurrection. Allah giveth without stint to whom He will.

S. II, v. 212

...The life of this world is but comfort of illusion.

S. III, v. 185

Naught is the life of the world save a pastime and a sport. Better far is the abode of the Hereafter for those who keep their duty (to Allah). Have ye then no sense?

S. VI, v. 32

Wealth and children are an ornament of life of the world. But the good deeds which endure are better in thy Lord's sight for reward, and better in respect of hope.

S. XVIII, v. 46

And whatsoever ye have been given is a comfort of the life of the world and an ornament thereof; and that which Allah hath is better and more lasting. Have ye then no sense?

S. XXVIII, v. 60

This life of the world is but a pastime and a game. Lo! the home of the Hereafter—that is Life, if they but knew.

S. XXIX, v. 64

Now whatever ye have been given is but a passing comfort for the life of the world, and that which Allah hath is better and more lasting for those who believe and put their trust in their Lord.

S. XLII, v. 36

And they say: There is naught but our life of the world; we die and we live, and naught destroyeth us save time; when they have no knowledge whatsoever of (all) that; they do but guess.

S. XLV, v. 24

The life of the world is but a sport and pastime. And if ye believe and ward off (evil), He will give you your wages, and will not ask of you your wordly wealth.

S. XLVII, v. 36

Know that the life of this world is only play, and idle talk, and pageantry, and boasting among you, and rivalry in respect of wealth and children; as the likeness of vegetation after rain, whereof the growth is pleasing to the husbandman, but afterward it drieth up and thou seest it turning yellow, then it becometh straw. And in the Hereafter there is grievous punishment, and (also) forgiveness from Allah and His good pleasure, whereas the life of the world is but matter of illusion.

S. LVII, v. 20

Rivalry in worldly increase distracteth you
Until ye come to the graves.
Nay, but ye will come to know!
Nay, but ye will come to know!
Nay, would that ye knew (now) with a sure knowledge!
For ye will behold hell-fire.
Aye, ye will behold it with sure vision.
Then, on that day, ye will be asked concerning pleasure.

S. CII, vv. 1-8

LIFE HEREAFTER—IMMORTALITY

...those who keep their duty to their Lord, for them are Gardens underneath which rivers flow, wherein they will be safe for ever. A gift of welcome from their Lord. That which Allah hath in store is better for the righteous.

S. III, v. 198

And as for those who believe and do good works, We shall make them enter Gardens underneath which rivers flow—to dwell therein for ever...

S. IV, v. 57

But (as for) those who believe and do good works—We tax not any soul beyond its scope—Such are rightful owners of the Garden. They abide therein.

S. VII, v. 42

And Allah summoneth to the abode of peace, and leadeth whom He will to a straight path.

For those who do good is the best (reward) and more (thereto). Neither dust nor ignominy cometh near their faces. Such are rightful owners of the Garden; they will abide therein.

S. X, vv. 25, 26

Lo! those who believe and do good works and humble themselves before their Lord: such are rightful owners of the Garden; they will abide therein.

S. XI, v. 23

Lo! those who say: Our Lord is Allah, and afterward are upright, the angels descend upon them, saying: Fear not nor grieve, but hear good tidings of the paradise which ye are promised.

We are your protecting friends in the life of the world and in the Hereafter. There ye will have (all) that your souls desire, and there ye will have (all) for which ye pray.

A gift of welcome from the Forgiving, the Merciful.

S. XLI, vv. 30-32

Thou seest the wrong-doers fearful of that which they have earned, and it will surely befall them; while those who believe and do good works (will be) in flowering meadows of the Gardens, having what they wish from their Lord. This is the great preferment.

S. XLII, v. 22

Now whatever ye have been given is but a passing comfort for the life of the world, and that which Allah hath is better and more lasting for those who believe and put their trust in their Lord.

S. XLII, v. 36

Lo! those who say: Our Lord is Allah, and thereafter walk aright, there shall no fear come upon them neither shall they grieve.

Such are rightful owners of the Garden, immortal therein, as a reward for what they used to do.

S. XLVI, vv. 13, 14

(And) lo! those who believe and do good works are the best of created beings.

Their reward is with their Lord: Gardens of Eden underneath which rivers flow, wherein they dwell for ever. Allah hath pleasure in them and they have pleasure in Him. This is (in store) for him who feareth his Lord.

S. XCVIII, vv. 7, 8

A CLOSING SURAH

The Unity

Say: He is Allah, the One!
Allah, the eternally Besought of all!
He begetteth not nor was begotten.
And there is none comparable unto Him.

S. CXII, vv. 1-4

Arberry renders this tremendous Surah as follows:

Sincere Religion

Say: He is God, One,
God, the Everlasting Refuge,
who has not begotten, and has not been begotten,
and equal to Him is not any one.

Pickthall says: this Surah has been called the essence of the Koran, of which it is really the last Surah.

40

AN INVOCATION

...Our Lord! Condemn us not if we forget, or miss the mark! Our Lord! Lay not on us such a burden as Thou didst lay on those before us! Our Lord! Impose not on us that which we have not the strength to bear! Pardon us, absolve us and have mercy on us, Thou, our Protector, and give us victory over the disbelieving folk.

S. II, v. 286

EPILOGUE:

INVITATION TO THE STUDY OF THE GLORIOUS QURAN

It is our hope that this short anthology may serve to stimulate interest in the study of the Glorious Quran. It is best read in Arabic—the language in which it was revealed 1400 years ago. For every Muslim, of course, it is mandatory to do so.

The Quran is a book of guidance for mankind. It enables man to discriminate between truth and falsehood. 'The great theophany of Islam', says Frithjof Schuon, 'is the Quran; it presents itself as being a discernment *(Furqan)* between truth and error. In a sense the whole of the Quran, one of the names of which is 'Al-Furqan' (Discernment), is a sort of multiple paraphrase of the fundamental discernment expressed by the *Shahadah* (The testimony of faith, i.e., there is no God but God and Muhammad is His Messenger). Its whole content is summed up in the words: Truth has come and error *(elbatil,* the empty or the inconsistent) has vanished away; verily error is ephemeral' (Surah XVII v. 73).[1]

The substance of the Quran comprises verses which are referred to as *'Muhakamat'* but there are others called *'Mutshabahat'*. The former are clear, unambiguous, direct statements and can be easily understood, but the latter are couched in the form of allegorical symbolism and their meaning is not easy to comprehend. The Quran itself says of this latter class of verses that 'those in whose hearts is doubt pursue, forsooth, that which is allegorical seeking (to cause) dissension by seeking to explain it. None knoweth its explanation save Allah. And those who are of sound instruction say: We believe therein; the whole is from our Lord; but only men of understanding really heed' (Surah III, v. 7). The believer must try to abide by the clear and decisive verses of the Quran, obeying the injunctions contained therein, which are clear-cut and precise; but where the

---

[1] See Frithjof Schuon, *Understanding Islam,* p. 43 (1976, Mandala Edition) Unwin Paperbacks.

verses are allegorical one should not try to impose upon the symbolism used interpretations of one's own anthropomorphic contrivance, something not discernible by those who have received knowledge from the Lord concerning them. The more one strives to live by the clear-cut commands of the Quran, the more one is helped by Divine Guidance to grasp the meaning of the esoteric verses of the Holy Book.

Although there are numerous translations of the Quran in English and other world languages, it is impossible for any one to claim that the original has been adequately translated in any language. Indeed, it is generally recognised that the Quran cannot be translated. There are good reasons for it. All translations, on a deeper study, turn out to be an inevitable intermixture of the verbal meaning suggested by the Arabic words used in the Book and the interpretation the translator places upon those words as he sees them being conditioned by their context, limited in his view by his terrestrial environment and by his own power of comprehension. The difficulty arises, as Schuon points out, because of 'the incommensurable disproportion between the Spirit and the limited resources of human language: it is as though the poverty-striken coagulation which is the language of mortal man were under the formidable pressure of the Heavenly Word broken into a thousand fragments, or as if God, in order to express a thousand truths, had but a dozen words at his command and so was compelled to make use of allusions heavy with meaning, of ellipses, abridgements and symbolical syntheses'.

The Quran is the one miracle on which the Prophet of Islam took his stand that he was God-Inspired. The Quran itself challenges the detractors of the Prophet to produce a Surah like that contained in it if their contention, that it is not the word of God but merely the speech of a mortal man, is true (Surah II, vv. 23, 24). The one compelling reason why one should believe in the prophetic mission of Muhammad (may God's peace be upon him) is that he brought this Divinely inspired revelation to mankind. The Quran points out in Surah XXV—The Criterion— vv. 1, 4-6.

---

1 See F. Schuon, pp. 44, 45.

Blessed is He Who hath revealed unto His slave the Criterion (of right and wrong), that he may be a warner to the
peoples.

Those who disbelieve say: This is naught but a lie that he
hath invented, and other folk have helped him with it, so
that they have produced a slander and a lie.

And they say: Fables of the men of old which he hath had
written down so that they are dictated to him morn and
evening.

Say (unto them, O Muhammad): He Who knoweth the
secret of the heavens and the earth hath revealed it. Lo! He
ever is Forgiving, Merciful.

This is a recurring refrain in the Quran, reminding mankind
that it is a Divine revelation.

The Quran confirms pre-existing revelations like the Torah
and the Gospel (Surah III, v. 3). It is 'a Reminder unto
believers' (Surah VII, v. 2). As would appear from the
Chapter on the Quran, it is also 'an exhortation' to mankind
from the Lord to ward off evil, and 'a balm for that which
is in the breasts, a guidance and a mercy for believers'
(Surah X, v. 57). It is 'full of blessing', (Surah XXXVIII,
v. 29). All these attributes which the Quran ascribes to the
Holy Word can be directly experienced if the believer were
to read the Sacred Book over and over again with that
sense of profound humility which is characteristic of those
who have faith in that what they are reading is the Message
from the Lord of the heavens and the earth, their Creator.

So much reverence is shown by the believers to the Holy
Book that it is impossible to convey an idea of it to any one
who is not steeped in Muslim tradition. It occupies a special
place in every Muslim home and is held in somewhat of
awe, intermingled with deep reverence and affection. When
some one is seen reciting the Quran one is not so much as
allowed to turn one's back towards it. Similarly when one
hears the Quran one has to listen to it attentively and, at
the end of the recitation, say that what has been heard
represents God's own Truth.

The spirit and manner in which 'Al-Quran' has to be read
impose upon the reader certain constraints. These, to begin

with, appear as an aspect of self-imposed discipline, but later they tend to become an overt manifestation of what is a natural disposition with which human beings are endowed to regard reverentially all manifestations of the Divine. It is an indispensible condition of being beneficially influenced by the Holy Word that we learn to approach it in a spirit of 'wise passiveness'—just listen to it, ponder it and not project into it the vain imaginings of our subjective consciousness.

The Quran is the Word of God, sent to mankind through the Prophet of Islam. To know that the words one reads in the Quran are God's Words is to prepare in one's innermost being an awareness of the Divine Presence.

After we have read again and again verses of the Quran with due devotion and receptivity and have meditated upon them, a psychic transformation begins to take place within our being—as though the Word of God was acting as an alchemy to change the base metal in us into gold. When we recite the verses that were first recited by the Prophet of Islam, their sound reverberates in the deepest recesses of our being and enables us to get some of the impact of the original call that came to the Prophet fourteen centuries ago, of which our own recitation from the Quran is only a faint and feeble echo.

The believers who approach the Quran in a spirit of humility and read it lovingly feel as though peace has descended upon them, and indeed the Quran warns man that unless he engages himself in constant remembrance of his Lord there is no way for him to find that inward peace his soul yearns for.

The Quran is a Sacred Book 'which none toucheth save the purified' (Surah LVI, v. 79). This is both an admonition to heed as also a condition precedent to the reader being at all in a position to have access to the meaning of the Quran. It is couched in the form of a warning that the believer has to be in a state of ritual purity before he can so much as touch the Holy Book. We are thus asked to approach it only when we are outwardly pure and inwardly humble and penitent. And it is only when we approach it thus that our humanity reaches a high water mark of excellence. Indeed it is then, if we are Divinely blessed and so endowed, that we present ourselves to God's Light, God who is the Light of all Universe, as a worthy medium for it to pass through to illumine the lives of our fellow beings in an ever widening circle till it transforms the world.

This selection of verses from Pickthall's universally well-known translation, *The Glorious Koran,* seeks to provide the essence of the Quranic message and to dispel many of the current misconceptions about Islam. Arranged thematically, the selection highlights the Holy Quran's pronouncements on man's role in the world, what is required of the true believers in daily conduct and prayer, stressing the qualities of truth, justice, humility, kindness and tolerance. The chapters on Jesus and the People of the Scripture show how closely Islam is related to Judaism and Christianity.

The merit of this selection is that it makes the Quran readily accessible to those who wish to understand the basic tenets of Islam. It is also the compiler's hope that his anthology will provide a source of spiritual inspiration amongst the distractions, pressures and crises of modern life, and lead the contemplative reader on to the Glorious Quran itself.

Aziz Ahmed has had a long and distinguished career in government, joining the Indian Civil Service in 1930 and after Partition, serving successively as Pakistan's Secretary to the Cabinet, Commerce Secretary, Secretary General, Ambassador to the USA, Foreign Secretary and, in the 1970s, Minister of State for Defence and Foreign Affairs, Foreign Minister and Senator until the declaration of Martial Law in 1977. He is a recipient of the highest Civil award, Hilal-i-Pakistan.

OXFORD UNIVERSITY PRESS   ISBN 0 19 577280 6